Nirupama Dutt is a poet, journalist and translator based in Chandigarh. She writes in Punjabi and English. Her published work includes *Ik Nadi Sanwali Jahi* (A Stream Somewhat Dark), a book of poems, for which she received the Punjabi Akademi Award; *Lal Singh Dil: Poet of the Revolution*, a translation of Dil's memoirs and poetry; *Stories of the Soil*, an anthology of Punjabi fiction; and *Half the Sky*, an anthology of fiction by Pakistani women writers. She has also translated *Pluto*, a book of Gulzar's short poems. At present, she is translating three novellas by the iconic Punjabi writer Amrita Pritam, and is working on a novel of her own.

The Ballad of
BANT SINGH
A QISSA OF COURAGE

NIRUPAMA DUTT

SPEAKING TIGER PUBLISHING PVT. LTD
4381/4 Ansari Road, Daryaganj,
New Delhi–110002, India

Copyright © Nirupama Dutt 2016

ISBN: 978-93-85755-28-6
eISBN: 978-93-85755-27-9

10 9 8 7 6 5 4 3 2 1

Typeset in Adobe Jenson Pro Capt by SÜRYA, New Delhi
Printed at Sanat Printers, Kundli

All rights reserved.
No part of this publication may be reproduced,
transmitted, or stored in a retrieval system, in any form or
by any means, electronic, mechanical, photocopying,
recording or otherwise, without the prior
permission of the publisher.

This book is sold subject to the condition that it shall not,
by way of trade or otherwise, be lent, resold, hired out,
or otherwise circulated, without the publisher's
prior consent, in any form of binding or cover
other than that in which it is published.

*This book is dedicated to the revolutionary
Dalit poet of Punjab, Sant Ram Udasi,
whose songs gave Bant Singh the strength to sing,
fight and live with dignity*

Of Bant We Sing...

Yes, in Punjab, we love to sing
But today we will sing not
Of 'old and distant unhappy things'
Nor of 'battles long ago'—
We will sing, yes we will sing, of
This day, of the here and the now
Of those who refused to bow
Those who can tell us how
Songs of hope are born in want
Why some can have it all
Why some cannot.
We will sing of the girl
Whose dreams died young
But who still wants justice done
And asks for a pistol in her dowry.
We will sing not of prejudice
But of the pride of a man
To fight for what is right
To keep his spirit always alive
To rise phoenix-like and say:
'Come let us all invoke Bhagat Singh.'
We will sing not of lost crowns
Landlords' sons, or a banished king
Today we will sing of Bant Singh...

Contents

Season of the Mustard Flower	1
The Night of 5 January	17
Before and After	41
The Long Road to Mansa	65
The Colour Violet	79
The Making of a Movement	113
Song Sung Red	139
The Inheritance of Caste	159
Iconoclast as Icon	187
Songs That Bant Sings	203
Select Bibliography	212
A Word of Thanks	213

Season of the Mustard Flower

Mother Earth! Many more Moons to your lap
Keep shining, O bright Sun, on the huts of labourers

—Udasi

'COME WHEN YOU can. I will be here to meet you, fresh as a flower in a mustard field.' Bant Singh's voice—loud and clear on the telephone—has a quality which tells me that the sun must be shining brightly upon his hut. He seems to be the chosen of Mother Earth, a force who overcame the storms which threatened his very existence.

Bant Singh has been described by the media as 'a singing torso', a terse but apt epithet. He has no arms and only one leg which, though saved from amputation, hangs lifelessly. He is dependent on many people for his existence. Yet he sings songs of protest like never before, each as fresh as a new blossom.

When I first meet Bant Singh in his village of Burj Jhabbar in the Mansa district of Punjab's Malwa region—the Cotton Belt—the mustard is in bloom. Tiny yellow flowers dot the landscape, as if a painting by Paramjit Singh has come to life and has broken the confines of its frame to fill acres of land. I have travelled through the Punjab countryside from the mid-seventies onwards, when the Green Revolution was at its bounteous best, and I have always looked upon the lushness with joy. But, now, the colour is shot through with grey.

The Ballad of Bant Singh

It seems grey this time, of all the others in particular, as I am in Malwa is to meet the widows of farmers who have committed suicide under the burden of agricultural debt. The months before the harvest in Punjab are called 'mitha mausam', the sweet season. The weather is cool, there is no work in the fields, it is time to eat jaggery and wait for a harvest of plenty. This is also a time of fairs and festivals. But the fairs and festivals have lost some of their sheen as addiction and agrarian crises are on the rise. Hearing one sorrowful story after another, of farmers consuming pesticide in the districts of Sangrur, Bathinda and Mansa, I reach a village where the widow of a Jat has been left destitute. Her two school-going sons do not even have shoes. She rears buffaloes in her home for a dairy and receives a small remuneration in return. 'My younger son says, "Ma let's die too, we don't even have chappals", but I tell him, "No son, never think of dying, we shall live even if it means walking barefoot."'

The assertion of life in the face of death and deprivation is reaffirmed more strongly when we get to Bant's house. His newly built brick-and-mortar dwelling with plastered walls and a proper kitchen, faces the fields, but is very much in the vehra, the part of villages in Punjab where the Dalits—known in the state as Mazhabi Sikhs—live. The vehra is on the outskirts of the village, traditionally at the western end so that the rays of the sun are not contaminated by the 'untouchables' before reaching the dwellings of the upper castes. The drainage also usually runs from east to west. There are some villages where the practice of situating the vehra in the west is not adhered to, but it is invariably the rundown, overcrowded and seamy side of the community.

The caste divide is geographically pronounced in most villages and different castes have separate residential areas. Usually, caste identification is the most unprompted beginning of any rural interaction: 'Tussi kihna de ho?' (Where do you belong?). Once one's caste has been declared, one will be placed in the given hierarchy and, needless to say, treated accordingly. Bhakti poet Kabir said, 'Jaat na poocho saadhu ki, pooch leejiye gyaan' (Ask not the caste of a saint but ask about his knowledge). Denunciation of caste was primary in the philosophy of Guru Nanak, the first Sikh Guru, too, and this is underlined in his hymn:

> Neechan andar neech jati, neechi hun ati neech
> Nanak tin ke sang sath, vadian siyon kya rees
> Jithe neech sanmanian, tithe nadr teri bakhshish
>
> I come from the lowest of the low castes, low, entirely low
> I am a friend to the lowly, not to the so-called high
> The blessings of God come to those who care for the low

The Ballad of Bant Singh

These illuminating words uttered centuries ago have not brought light to a society deeply and very selfishly entrenched in caste.

Yet, the pull which the village exerts on all of its residents is strong. Dalit fiction writer Attarjit probes the complexity of this attachment in his autobiography *Akk da Dudh* (Poison Milk):

> The soil of my village was no more special than any other yet it had the power to pull me like nothing else and fill my senses with elation. However, I never experienced here what poets call 'fragrance of earth'. Perhaps such phrases are just poetic euphemisms. Ever since I can recall I just saw filth and more filth all around: small and dirty mud tenements. Outside, there was slush and water in unpaved drains that were the abode of creepy-crawly insects. A little beyond were mounds of dirt and garbage as well as the prevailing stench of human urine and excreta.

In Burj Jhabbar, fifty-five per cent of the population is Jat and forty-five Dalit. There are only two other castes in the village: two Bania brothers who are shopkeepers, and two houses belonging to families of the Jheevar or water-bearer caste. The neighbouring villages provide the other facilities or skills needed in Burj Jhabbar. Most of the Dalits in this village—which was jointly set up by the Jats and Dalits of Aklia village not more than two hundred years ago—are agrarian labourers. It has a total population of around fifteen hundred. Almost one or two Dalit youths from each family work as attached labourers with the Jats at abominally low wages of eighteen to twenty thousand rupees per annum. Only five Dalits of the village have government jobs and that too of the Class III or Class IV variety. There is one retired army jawan but his sons too are working as attached labourers. The Dalit tenements are shabby. Earlier, Bant too lived in a tenement of loose bricks held together by mud. However, his new home has two pukka rooms—though doors still have to be added—a verandah, a kitchen and some open space. This was made possible from money raised by sympathetic supporters and media organizations.

Accompanying me on this first visit to the Dalit singer's house are two acquaintances from Mansa: poet Gurpreet and senior Left-wing activist and leader of the Democratic Employees Front of Punjab, Sukhdarshan Natt. The latter has been a part of the long struggle and agony of Bant Singh and is his mentor too. Jimmy, Bant Singh's black pet dog, barks a welcome and starts wagging his tail. We walk past the big buffaloes tied under the keekar tree which gives them shade. Bant is stretched out on a cot in the verandah. His young son helps him sit up. Bant then raises the stump of what was once his right arm and offers everyone a laal salaam, the red salute. With Bant's gesture, the near-forgotten charm of the laal salaam returns. Very few people use this greeting with genuineness anymore. It is now a cliché and, at times, a gesture of derision. With Bant Singh, there is nothing hollow about the laal salaam; he believes in it and he lives it.

I am reminded of another time when this salutation touched my heart, although it was in an incongruous setting. In the early nineties I visited Mai Banno's mazaar at Banur on the Chandigarh-Patiala road. The little shrine is dedicated to a washerwoman well versed in classical music which she had picked up just by sitting outside the house of a maestro. Legend has it that Tansen, scorched after singing Raag Deepak (the raag of the lamp) in Akbar's court, reached Banur. Here Mai Banno gave him water to drink and sang Raag Malhar (the raag of rain). Her singing brought clouds and rain to heal Tansen's singed body and soul. Every year a big langar, a community meal, is held in the mazaar. Once, I stopped to partake of it and most noticeable among the volunteers was an old Comrade, well over eighty, who served kadhi-chawal to visitors with a hearty laal salaam which had the same genuine ring of Bant Singh's welcome.

What does the laal salaam mean to Bant? He smiles. 'The red salute links me to every worker in the country. In this greeting, red is for the blood that flows through the veins of a labourer; the blood that a worker is not afraid to shed in struggle. You know the red of the Communist flag means the same. The flag was first white, but the blood of the workers dyed it red.' After this simply and surely put reply, Bant moves on to discuss the activities of the Mazdoor Mukti Morcha of the All India Agricultural Labour Association (AIALA), associated with the CPI Marxist-Leninist (CPI M-L) Liberation Party. This overground Party evolved from a faction of the ML and it now participates in the democratic process of the country with representation in state assemblies. Word gets around that Bant has visitors from Mansa; some elders from the neighbourhood come calling and settle down on charpais in the courtyard.

As the discussion warms up, a tall, slim and attractive girl brings steaming hot tea. A little boy is trailing her. Natt, patting the child on his head, tells me, 'This is Baljit, Bant Singh's eldest daughter.' I am silent for a moment, then force a smile on to my lips as I look at this young mother who is barely out of girlhood. Her testimony echoes in my ears: 'I, Baljit Kaur, daughter of Shri Bant Singh, am a resident of Burj Jhabbar in Mansa district, Punjab. I was gang-raped on July 6, 2002. I did not conceal the incident and along with my father waged a struggle for justice…' I wonder if I will ever be able to talk to her about her travails. The idea that she would have to relive her pain all over again is horrendous to me. I was to realize later that my hesitation arose from the comfort of my own relatively privileged existence. Those who are pushed to the wall find the courage to tell their tale of woe over and again.

Bant Singh's was that rare case in which a Dalit had defied the sarpanch of a village to seek justice in a court and had succeded in having the culprits sentenced to life imprisonment. And, for this, he and his family had to pay a very heavy price. This was because a Dalit had actually succeeded in getting an upper-caste Jat man and two others convicted of rape.

What, after all, does a Dalit labourer have? He has neither money nor influence. All he has is his own body, which he must use to earn a livelihood. And, as for the body of the Dalit woman, it is very easy for it to be seen as an object of casual, easy abuse. In Bant's case, and in Baljit's, it was their bodies which became the sites of oppression.

There was this very crude joke that a Jat boyfriend told me many years ago when we were classmates at the School of Journalism in Panjab University. 'In the village we laugh that if you make out with an "untouchable" girl [the word Dalit was not in vogue at that time in our part of the country] you get defiled and then you have to make out with a Brahmin girl for purification's sake!' At nineteen I just dismissed it as a rustic off-colour joke without realizing that I was probably being considered a potential agent of purification.

Season of the Mustard Flower

Jokes are not born in a vacuum and we laugh at what is perhaps the most painful and appalling of our realities. I remember someone recalling one of our upper-caste, haloed revolutionary poets, who enjoys a 'martyr' status in the Left universe—and in some Right circles too—as he was killed in the days of terrorism in Punjab. I was told that he had confided in his friends that his greatest thrill was the scream of a Dalit girl when he violated her. More recently, I overheard the conversation of a young journalist colleague who was boasting how he and his cousin raped a mother and daughter who came to sweep their house. He even went on to recount that they had their fill as the two women kept whimpering: 'Brother, please don't... Let us be, brother...' Their pleas found no ears nor did the address of 'brother' soften the men's hearts.

The rape of a Dalit girl is accepted as a coming-of-age ritual for a Jat boy. The stories and myths vary from district to district, but the ultimate aim is the same: the exploitation of the Dalit girl. The more 'cultured' upper-caste sons of the soil do not normally talk about this, but it takes only two drinks for them to start boasting of the times they have 'done' a Dalit girl.

The rape of a Dalit girl makes for a brief report in a newspaper and it is soon forgotten. According to the Indian Human Rights Report, 2007, Dalit women in Punjab were easy targets of violence and sexual abuse by

The Ballad of Bant Singh

the upper castes. It reported cases that had appeared in newspapers. Among the cases was one of a teenaged Dalit girl of Kot Todar Mal village who was gang-raped for four days by three upper-caste youths. On 17 February 2006, three backward-caste women, Amarjit, Virpal and Rani, were stripped, beaten and given electric shocks by the police for refusing to gratify two upper-caste men of Johar village in Muktsar district. Such crimes are an everyday affair in the villages, towns and cities of Punjab. Rarely are the guilty punished, because most victims do not have the resources to pursue their cases. At other times, some compromise is arrived at and the charges are withdrawn.

So a Dalit girl and her father who came out in the open to seek justice, and resisted considerable pressure and temptation in doing so, are unusual and brave. Bant Singh, an ordinary Dalit singer of revolutionary songs, who was little known except at workers' rallies in the districts of the Cotton Belt, accomplished the extraordinary. His success was unpalatable to many.

~

The evening is fast approaching and Bant Singh's daughter lights the earthen stove in the courtyard. He insists that we stay for dinner, but his comrades decline the invitation as we have to move on. Bant is well known for his culinary skills and comrades from the party office relish the simple but delicious fare cooked in his house. Bant says: 'They tell me, when our party comes to power, we will build a hotel for Bant to run. I can no longer stir the pot but my daughters have learnt to cook food with just the right amount of cumin and coriander. The salt is never less and never more, so is the case with all other spices. Each dish has to be cooked its own special way.' He explains that he inherited the love of cooking from his mother Bachan Kaur, whom he is said to resemble. 'When we would get up, food would be cooked and ready. On some special days a rich aroma would hover in the open kitchen in the courtyard. Mother would feed us deer meat or wild boar which someone had brought back as shikar and shared with everyone.'

The neighbours take leave and, as we linger, Bant decides the menu. He then instructs his third son, Manjit, to get some potatoes from a shop in the village as the dish for the evening meal is aloo-matar. I think of a line from a poem by Kumar Vikal, a modern Hindi poet from Punjab: 'Aloo-matar ki sabzi ek gharib Punjabi ki sabse ameer sabzi hai' (A meal of potatoes-and-peas is the richest dish of a poor Punjabi).

Bant's youngest daughter Hardeep, who I later find out would rather be studying than doing household chores, starts shelling peas. Sukhminder, the pretty third daughter who never went to school because she started helping her ailing mother with house work when she was but a small girl, starts grinding a paste of fresh ginger, garlic and onions in an earthen pot. Bant instructs: 'Fry the paste until it is light brown and then toss the potatoes in. Add the peas only when you are adding the water.' He is giving Sukhminder lessons in good cooking because he is looking for a match for her.

The subject of this book is gently brought up and I tell Bant that I will be coming again to meet him. With true Punjabi largesse he replies, 'Come whenever you want and stay for as long as you want. This is your own house.'

Gurpreet, Natt and I drive back through mustard fields where millions of yellow flowers sparkle in the rays of the setting sun. In the words of Kumar Vikal:

> In phoolon ko koi guldaste mein nahi sajayega
> Koi ladhki ihne apne taaza dhule baalon mein nahi lagayegi
> Par inki mehak bahut door tak mere saath jaayegi...
>
> No one will arrange these flowers in a vase
> No girl will adorn her freshly washed hair with these blooms
> But their fragrance will travel a long way with me...

It was Vikal who first showed me the way out of an elite lifestyle; a means to become one with those who toil, struggle, smile and sing—never mind if they are often dismissed as the wretched of the earth. The years spent writing the story of Bant were an intense journey, replete with poetry and pain.

As we drive, accompanied by the fragrance, I realize that my journey through Punjab is never to be the same again. The sad and violent secrets of human existence linger in the picturesque countryside. 'How can such ugliness co-exist with the innocent beauty of the ruralscape?' I wonder, as I collect bits and pieces about Bant's life, as well as the lives of many like him. 'I hope Bant is safe in the open like this?' I ask and Natt laughs at the naiveté of my question. 'What more can they do to him? Kill him? But they will not, for they have perhaps realized that it may not be so easy to play with the lives of the oppressed. The oppressed will rise and question injustice.'

My first visit to Bant was at an end but I was left wondering how I would play Boswell to him. This was a new territory that I was entering, one paved with misery, but one which Bant and his people gradually eased my way into it. The untravelled path has its lows and one sometimes stumbles or sinks into deep depression but, most of the time, one is elated by the courage and resilience that comes to the fore.

This, then, is the ballad of Bant Singh.

The Night of 5 January

Peddlers of gloom, radiance is never vanquished;
O killers of sunshine, the sun is never extinguished

—Udasi

THE NIGHT OF 5 January in 2006 saw the peddlers of gloom prowling about in the green fields near Burj Jhabbar to ensure that darkness should be the lot of a people who, silenced and enslaved for centuries, were now daring to raise their voice. Not just raise their voice but challenge and seek justice from the law of the land. This must change, the oppressors told themselves, pouring country liquor down their throats. Those who had dared to change the established order of their lives had to be taught a lesson.

When Bant Singh cycled from his home in the afternoon of 5 January, he was not out on some great mission. Nor did he know what the dark, cold night held in store for him. In his pocket were pamphlets for an upcoming Party rally, ready to be distributed, and a few crisp hundred-rupee notes to buy some special treats for his children. The agrarian festival of Lohri was just a week away. Lohri is a truly Punjabi festival. Diwali has its fireworks and fun but, for Punjabis, Lohri marks the end of the bitingly cold winter and the sowing of crops to be harvested a few months later. Preparations were afoot in his village for the festival. The women had started slapping down dung cakes in advance for the cooking. Firewood had been stacked so that the customary bonfire would last late into the night. Bant's second daughter, Paramjit, had made a cow-dung image of the Goddess Lohri and the younger children were busy practising Lohri songs—in a few days they would go to homes in the village with gifts of popcorn, peanuts and jaggery sweets. It is considered inauspicious to send the children away empty-handed. If someone is brave or desperate enough to do so, the little ones hurl the ultimate insult and that too in rhyme: 'Hukka bhai hukka! Eh ghar bhukha', meaning that the household is so impoverished that it cannot give away even a few festive savouries.

The day was bright and sunny. The mid-day meal had been the traditional sarson da saag and makki di roti. Basking in a patch of the sun outside his house, Bant Singh was surrounded by his three younger children: the studious Hardeep and Manjit and, the youngest, the family's darling, Paroche. Paroche was being taught the Lohri song for he would be doing the rounds of the village this time. Resting his head on his father's arm, he repeated the song his father recited:

> Sunder mundriye ho!
> Tera kaun vicharaa ho!
> Dulla Bhatti walla ho!

The Night of 5 January

> Beautiful girl
> Who will care for you
> But for Dulla Bhatti

Hardeep, ever inquisitive, cut short the chorus of 'Ho!' and asked her father: 'Bhapaji, tell me who Dulla Bhatti was.'

'You are in Class IV and don't even know who Dulla Bhatti was?' Manjit taunted his older sister.

Bant laughed and stroked Manjit's head, 'My boy, you are in Class III, you tell your sister who he was?'

'He was a very big dacoit!'

'Wrong, my son. He was a leader of poor peasants and he robbed the greedy rich only to feed the needy poor.'

The children listened, all attention, as Bant told the story of Punjab's own Robin Hood. Dulla, the leading man of Lohri festivities and a much celebrated folk hero, buried at the Miani Sahib Qabristan in Lahore, lived during the early years of the reign of Mughal emperor Akbar. It is said he was a Muslim Rajput of the Bhatti clan who led a guerilla revolt against the tyranny of the zamindars. He was also the saviour of poor girls whose future was merely to be sold in the slave market. He would adopt these girls and arrange their marriages. Thus went the age-old song to Dulla:

> Dulle dhee viyai ho!
> Ser shakkar paayi ho!

The Ballad of Bant Singh

Kudhi da laal pachaka ho!
Kudhi da saalu paatta ho!
Saalu kaun samete ho!
Chache choori kutti ho!
Zamindara lutti ho!

Dulla married off his daughter
He gave her a measure of sugar
The girl dressed in bridal red
Her shawl is torn
Who will mend her shawl?
Her uncle makes sweet bread
The landlords loot it all.

'Why was her shawl torn?' Hardeep wanted to know.

For once, Bant had no ready reply. He did not see a torn red shawl but the violet suit his own daughter had been wearing, and which had been ripped apart. How was he to tell young Hardeep why and how the shawl was torn? He felt restless. How long had this been going on and how long would it continue? The next question came from Manjit: 'Why did the zamindars loot the choori?'

Bant smiled—the sweet choori was just a metaphor for everything that the landlords plundered. 'The zamindars loot not just the choori but our labour, our honour, our pride, our very existence!'

Bant's wife, Harbans, was sensitive to her husband's slightest change of mood. She put her hand on her

The Night of 5 January

husband's and said, 'Now stop this daytime story-telling.' Then she turned to chide Hardeep and Manjit: 'Let your father be. Your grandmother used to say that one must not listen to stories in the daytime or else your uncle will forget the way to our home. Who then will bring tasty goodies for you?'

Hardeep and Manjit went away but the youngest one still clung to his father.

'Don't fret so much. We have to move on with life for the sake of our children,' she said, pressing Bant's hand softly.

'You are right, Harbans, but how long will we keep suffering? Things have to change.'

Harbans wanted to calm him, to reassure him that she would always be by his side. 'Things will change and we will continue to fight, but let us be happy, for it is festival time. Tell me, which sweets should we prepare for Lohri?'

Hardeep and Manjit heard the word 'sweets' and came jumping back to their parents.

'What will you make this time, Bibi? I want to eat gajar da halwa,' Hardeep said, hugging her mother.

'I want to eat pinni. Yesterday, Chachi's son had brought pinni to school in his tiffin-box.'

Paroche, lifting his head from his father's arms, settled the matter by declaring: 'I want both gajar da halwa and pinni.'

The Ballad of Bant Singh

This brought laughter all around and, getting up from the charpai, Bant swung Paroche in his arms and said: 'Okay Bachchoo, you will get both but I have to get khoya for your mother to prepare these delicacies. Harbans, I will go to Burj Dhilwan for khoya. Seva Singh told me the other day that you get very good khoya at the gurudwara there.'

'Don't go today. It is afternoon already. Go tomorrow morning. I don't like your being out late. I tell you, these people are after your life.' The village boys had attacked Bant twice in the previous year, but the police had taken scant notice of their complaints.

'O my brave woman, what has happened to you? Let me complete the task. You know I don't like putting off work for another day. I will come back before sunset,' Bant said and, soon, he was out, wearing his buff-coloured jacket and blue trousers, his red-turbaned head held high.

Bant liked to dress well and this was one of things about him which irked the Jat landlords. 'He doesn't look like a Choorha nor does he dress like one. He walks with the pride of someone well-born,' they would say resentfully.

Cycling down the metalled road, Bant stopped by the fields that once belonged to his grandfather Dhanna Singh. He smiled as he remembered how his grandfather would shout with pride: 'I will never work in anyone's

The Night of 5 January

fields.' Dhanna Singh's grandchildren would repeat the words, little realizing that this was something that was easier said than done—tillers are rarely allowed to own land. How his people had suffered for thousands of years and continued to do so till today. 'So ridiculous that birth should decide the fate of a person!' Bant brooded. He told himself that he would struggle in every way to better their lot and his birth would not be in vain. He conjured up images of his two heroes, Guru Gobind Singh, the tenth Guru of the Sikhs, who founded the Khalsa and embraced an untouchable; and the patriot Bhagat Singh, who went smiling to the gallows at only twenty-three years of age. Stories of both these brave men were a constant inspiration to him. Although an activist of an ultra-Left Party and addressed as Comrade, he had no knowledge of Marx or Mao. The radicals of the Punjabi soil were his ideals.

~

Bant Singh was born in 1965 in a Mazhabi Sikh family. He was the seventh child of Jagir Singh and Bachan Kaur. A baby girl was born after him and, with eight children in all—four sons and four daughters—it was a full house. The chowkidar of villages came every few months to keep a record of births and deaths in villages and very often chose his own names when the family had not yet decided on a name for the newborn. The chowkidar settled on Santokh Singh but Dhanna Singh was not satisfied. He chose a name from the Sikh scriptures. Bant is a derivation from Beant, which means limitless, and is an attribute of God. Growing up unlettered amidst poverty, Bant nevertheless inherited the Sikh traditions of courage and self-esteem.

The family was devoutly Sikh and took pride in the fact that they were the chosen children of the tenth Guru of the Sikhs, Guru Gobind Singh, who had initiated them into the Khalsa.

Mazhabi literally means one who has a mazhab or a religion and remains steadfast to the faith. It is a very positive title, but is used with contempt because the Mazhabis are lowest in the caste hierarchy as laid down by Manu and which Hinduism has adhered to for centuries. Bant Singh's family were from the Choorha caste. Their counterparts in Hindi-speaking areas are called Bhangis, a community which has been bound by heredity to remain scavengers and sweepers. Thus they were at the bottom rung of the castes condemned as 'untouchable'. They were the village menials who were not allowed to enter religious spaces and their touch and even sight meant defilement to the Brahmins and other upper castes. While terms such as 'Choorha' and 'Bhangi' have been outlawed by the Consititution, they are still used by a large section of the population. These days, however, many Dalits feel no indignity in owning

The Night of 5 January

these caste names and, on the contrary, find the patronizing Gandhian tag of Harijan, people of God, more offensive.

Caste discrimination in the Hindu religion goes back to ancient times and has resulted in many reform movements, especially in the medieval era, that had as their aim the end of caste discrimination and the accommodation of the 'untouchables' in the Hindu fold. But these movements had limited success. Many people of the 'low' castes converted to Islam and Christianity, which have no concept of caste. However, the caste system travelled to Islam and Christianity, too, and to the other religions of the subcontinent, and the converts from the 'low' castes often found no dignity even in their new lives. With the exception of the Gurus, who practised what they preached, Sikhism has been no different.

Guru Nanak (1469-1539), the first Guru of the Sikhs, propagated the idea of the oneness of God and a casteless society. He was a social revolutionary and the very essence of his mission was the erasing of the caste system to embrace all of humanity. His followers came from different religions and castes, attracted by the new spiritual awakening that he offered. In his wide travels, accompanied by his close companion Mardana, who was a low-caste Muslim Mirasi, he set up sangats (congregations) where everyone would sit together to pray and meditate, irrespective of their religion, caste or creed. The second was the practice of sitting in a pangat (row) and eating together—the langar. Sangat, pangat and langar were the three essentials of the new faith.

The Dalits had come into the Sikh fold from the very beginning, with Nanak choosing Mardana as his constant companion and confidante. The fourth Guru, Ram Das (1534-1581), accepted Dalits as his followers, many of whom are still called Ramdasias. Nearly every Sikh Guru had Dalits among his followers. Guru Angad Dev (1504-1552) developed the practice of 'Guru ka langar' and his wife Mata Khiwi is much venerated because she dedicated her heart and soul to this institution. Legend has it that when the Mughal emperor Humayun visited Goindwal Sahib, he was asked to join the pangat for langar before meeting the Guru. In the philosophy of the Gurus, no one is high and no one low. In fact, while the Gurus came from upper castes, the lower castes—whom we refer to as Dalits in the present context—were an important segment of Sikhism. Significantly, the hymns of the three lower-caste exponents of the Bhakti movement—Kabir, Namdev and Ravi Das—are included in the Guru Granth Sahib, the holy book of the Sikhs, and for good reason. These were the poets who first openly critiqued the caste system.

Bant was but a child when he heard for the first time

The Night of 5 January

from his grandfather the story of how the tenth and the last living Guru of the Sikhs inducted the 'untouchables' as baptised Sikhs and warriors of the Khalsa force. The story of Bhai Jaita (1649-1705), a disciple of Gobind Singh, was well known, but hearing it as a child left a powerful impression upon Bant.

Bhai Jaita belonged to the Ranghar caste of scavengers. When Guru Tegh Bahadur, father of the tenth Guru, was beheaded in full public view at Chandni Chowk, Delhi, in November 1675, the fear was such that no one came forward to claim his mortal remains. Displaying exemplary courage, Bhai Jaita attacked the guards and placed the severed head of the Guru in a basket and covered it carefully. Then, braving a stormy night, he carried it to the Guru's bereaved son Gobind Singh at Anandpur Sahib in Punjab. Showering praise on Bhai Jaita, the young Gobind Singh cried out in admiration and gratitude: 'Ranghreta Guru ka beta' (The boy of the Ranghar caste is now the son of the Guru). Later, he was baptised as Khalsa by Guru Gobind Singh and given the name of Bhai Jiwan Singh. Bhai Jiwan Singh died fighting the Guru's last battle in 1705. Bant wanted to be as brave as Bhai Jaita and the Guru found a hallowed place in his young heart.

The emergence of Sikhism was a turning point for the lower castes in Punjab. Three of the Panj Piare (Five Beloved Ones) were from the backward classes. Bhai

The Ballad of Bant Singh

Himmat Rai was a water-carrier, Bhai Sahib Chand a barber and Bhai Mohkam Chand a washerman. The Dalit identity was submerged within the Sikh identity. As Punjabi Dalit historian Rajkumar Hans points out in his paper, 'Dalits and the Emancipatory Sikh Religion': 'In true egalitarian spirit, Sikhism had succeeded in integrating the lowliest of the low, the former untouchables, the Dalits, into its fold... The way Bhai Jaita was integrated not only into the Sikh religion but also into the family of Guru Gobind Singh, it is understandable any other identity would have been meaningless to him.'

Gobind Singh decided to found the Khalsa army at Anandpur Sahib in 1699 and asked for five people from among his followers who were ready to be beheaded at his command. There was a stunned silence but five volunteers did come forward, one by one. The Guru took them into a tent. The congregation assumed that the Guru had killed them but were surprised to see them emerge with him from the tent wearing resplendent robes. These five were the first to be initiated into the new order by drinking amrit, or divine nectar, made of water into which Mata Sahib Kaur, the Guru's wife, had stirred a few patasas with a double-edged dagger, the khanda. With this baptism they were declared khalsas, the pure ones. Then he asked them to baptise him, their Guru.

The Night of 5 January

Khushwant Singh writes in his book *The Sikhs*: 'Gobind's first five disciples included three who were of lower castes. With determined deliberation he said he would mix the four castes into one—like the four constituents of paan (betel leaf) which when chewed produces just one colour.' The names of all those who were initiated were suffixed with Singh (lion). This in itself was a great revolutionary act because until then only the privileged martial classes used the suffix. However, Singh points out that inequality remained because no marriage alliances were made with the Mazhabi Sikhs. And despite their good intentions, the Gurus could not mix the four castes into one because the prejudice was too deep-rooted. In the same book Khushwant Singh adds with reference to the realities of the present: 'Sikhism did not succeed in breaking the caste system. If intermarriage is considered the test of equality, at no time was there much intercaste marriage between Sikhs converted from different Hindu castes. The Untouchable converted to Sikhism remained an outcaste for matrimonial alliances. Although he was no longer untouchable in the sense of not being touched and sat in temples along with other Sikhs, in time...Sikhs of higher castes refused to eat with untouchable Sikhs and in villages separate wells were provided for them.' Today, cremation grounds in villages and small towns continue to be separate and the past decades have seen the rise of caste-based gurudwaras.

The Ballad of Bant Singh

Mazhabi Sikhs were never to get the self-esteem or the love that Gobind Singh had showered on the valiant Bhai Jaita. At best they remained, and still do, serfs to the privileged landed Jats and subjects of scorn for the upper castes.

However, Bant's grandfather Dhanna Singh never lost his self-respect and he would tell his young grandsons with pride, as they went out with him every day to graze goats, 'I have never worked and will never work on land that belongs to another.'

Recalling this, Bant laughed and said, 'We boys would raise our arms and echo his words, "Yes, we will never work on land that belongs to another!"'

This was certainly not an easy pledge to keep. Many of Dhanna Singh's grandsons—he had over a dozen—had to eat their own words. But not Bant, he never forgot the pledge. Bant was in many ways a Dhanna Singh all over again, having inherited his grandfather's mellifluous voice, courage and spirit to live a life better than the one forced upon him in the name of caste. After all, they were the Ranghreta—the true sons of the Guru. Witness to the open sexual explotation of Dalit women in his own village, Bant once lamented, 'As long as my grandfather was alive, no Jat boy dared enter the vehra looking for our girls.' Such was the gravitas Dhanna Singh possessed.

For Bant his goatherding days were the happiest in

The Night of 5 January

his life. Those were carefree days when the young cousins carried sticks and herded their goats out in the wild with their grandfather as their leader. It was work, but while the goats grazed, the boys played games or became a captive audience for their grandfather's singing. Old Dhanna Singh would sing qissas of Heer-Ranjha, Sassi-Punnu and Mirza-Sahiban, the ill-fated lovers of Punjab who perished fighting the social taboos that would not allow their union. Such was the power of his voice that it would echo all over.

'When the sun started moving west, we would start calling out to our goats. We gave them names: Kaale kaan wali bakri (the black-eared goat), Chitte kaan wali bakri (the white-eared one), Phulwali if she had a white patch on her forehead or Bhuri if she was brown.' On the way home Bant would wonder what his mother had cooked for supper—would he get chholey with roti or masari dal? But there were times when he would get a sound thrashing instead of food. 'Once, on a hot summer day, I had taken off my shirt while playing with my cousins and had forgotten to wear it as we made our way home. Another time my eldest sister, who was newly married, was visiting us. In the morning I picked up her dupatta and tied it round my head as a makeshift turban but lost it during play. So a sound slap awaited me because even in those days a dupatta cost as much as fifteen rupees,' he recounted.

The Ballad of Bant Singh

Bant's father worked as a peon at the Government School in Aklia, a village some seven kilometres from theirs, and only came home on Sundays and other holidays. But Bant had his grandfather. How Dhanna Singh, who belonged to a family of landless labourers, came to own land is a tale in itself.

After Independence, some twenty-five to thirty acres had been set aside by the government for allotment to landless labourers. But there were initial hurdles. Mukhtiar Singh, Bant's paternal uncle, whom Bant addresses affectionately as 'Member'—the old man had been a former member of the panchayat—recounted: 'The tehsildar wanted a bribe of three hundred rupees and was ready to allot all the thirty acres to us, but that was a huge sum and could not be raised by putting together all our combined resources. Wages those days meant some meagre share of grain from the landlords or some loose coins at the end of a day of back-breaking work. So only seven acres was given, of which my father Dhanna Singh's share was three-and-a-half.'

Right from childhood to youth to adulthood, Bant's life had been a constant struggle to better the lot of a people who had been condemned for no fault of their own to the most meagre of livelihoods. He had traversed a forty-year-long road but his determination had never flagged. It was anger at injustice that propelled him forward. Bant reflected that it was ironic that the Sikhs

The Night of 5 January

had themselves forgotten the essence of Sikhism: that there should be no discrimination among human beings.

~

Bant stood leaning on his cycle so lost in thought that he had forgotten he had some work in another village. His reverie was interrupted by the sound of an approaching motorbike. He turned and waved when he saw his namesake, Beant Akali, the friendly Jat landlord who had always stood by him. The motorbike came to a halt and Beant Akali shouted out in his usual brusque manner, 'O Bant, what are you doing standing by the fields. The wheat will not grow faster under your gaze. Or are you composing some new song?'

'No Bai, I am going to Burj Dhilwan for some work. I just stopped for a while.'

'Carry on and finish your work. I am going to Joga to meet some people. I hope those boys are not troubling you anymore. Come and see me tomorrow and we will discuss matters,' Beant said, kick-starting his motorbike.

Bant heaved a sigh and started pedaling. When he reached the vehra at Burj Dhilwan, he learnt that the friend he had come to meet had gone off on an errand somewhere. Bant sat down to talk to his friend's uncle, Seva Singh, and the latter's wife Gurjeet Kaur rushed off to heat some sweet, milky tea. This Dalit family was very grateful to Bant because he had freed them from the shackles of a debt to their landlords which the poor people had thought would end only with their death. Perhaps not even that, for their children would continue to be saddled with the burden. Some fifteen years earlier the couple had taken a loan of five thousand rupees for the wedding of Seva's sister. For the next eleven years they kept paying back the five thousand rupees and would have continued to do so for the rest of their lives. They had paid fifty-five thousand rupees in all but were still in debt because the Jat moneylender had two relatives in the police and the labourers were afraid to protest. Finally the Party intervened and, through Bant's negotiations, pressurized the moneylender into letting Seva Singh and his family off.

Bant had just put down the tumbler after drinking the tea when Seva, who was now one of the members of the Mazdoor Mukti Morcha, came home.

Bant hailed him with a laal salaam. 'Where were you? I have been waiting here.'

'Bai, I had just gone off to get some medicine for the old man. He has been coughing a lot of late,' Seva said and called out to his wife to bring some milk for the visitor.

'I have already had milk, don't bother,' Bant said, getting up, and added, 'we better get going. It is quite late and we have a lot of work. We have to distribute these pamphlets and then get some khoya from the gurudwara. Your sister-in-law needs it to make sweets

The Night of 5 January

for Lohri.' Seva wrapped a shawl around his shoulders and the two friends set off on the bicycle.

~

It was already six when Bant neared the fields around his village. He was happy because the pamphlets had been distributed and he was taking home two kilos of excellent khoya. Carrying it in his shoulder bag, he pedalled quickly. Harbans is a simple woman, he thought, who is always worrying about me. He was lucky to have found such a wife. His mind went back to the lovely round-faced bride she had been. She had looked so pretty in her flowery magenta suit and the matching dupatta covering her head. Time and illness had taken their toll on her. Her face was now gaunt and her body frail, but her love for him was as strong as ever.

Humming a line from a song, he turned into a narrow path between the fields. A little ahead he saw a group of people. 'Now what is this meeting that is happening so late in the evening?' he asked himself. He soon realized that these were the same boys who had attacked him twice earlier. 'The past few years have been more than difficult,' he thought, 'although difficulty dogs every step of a poor labourer's life.' Soon after the second assault he had stopped the boys from entering the Bania's house next door to his, where they had come to ogle his daughters. This had led to yet another quarrel.

The Ballad of Bant Singh

Bant Singh's humming was cut short because he understood that the boys had probably come back to settle scores. They must have seen him leave the village and were now lying in wait for him. He stopped and counted; there were seven men in the group. His anxiety mounted: there seemed no escape and there was no one else in sight. He prided himself on his strong body, and he could have fought off one or even perhaps two men, but how could he deal with seven young men hell bent on teaching him a lesson?

Quickly throwing his bicycle to one side of the path, he started running through the fields. But the youths had come well prepared. They followed him on their scooters and jeep and surrounded him. 'Why are you after me? Let me go, or you will suffer,' he shouted loudly, hoping to frighten them away. But there was no scaring them that evening. They had come well-armed and their hatred was emboldened by the country liquor which they had poured down their throats. They wanted to silence Bant for all time to come and make him an example for all the other Dalits who dared to challenge them. The boys had done their homework well. Since they didn't want to attract the charge of culpable homicide—which using sharp weapons would bring down upon them—they had brought along blunt weapons: the curved metal handles of handpumps.

Four of the boys dragged him to the edge of the

The Night of 5 January

irrigation canal. There they put his legs on the embankment wall. A rough cloth was thrown on him as four of the men pinned him down. Two raised the metal handles and brought them down with all their strength on his shins. The pain stunned Bant but he still tried to raise himself and shouted, 'What are you doing? What have I done for you to hit me?' One of the boys struck him with even greater force and hissed, 'We are just doing a job that has been assigned to us. Today, you will not get away!' Blow upon blow, and the bones of Bant Singh's legs were splintered beyond repair. Then, sure that Bant had been irretrievably incapacitated, they swung him about and began attacking his arms. 'So you won't let us enter the vehra… Does the village belong to you?' said one. '*You* will decide where we should play badminton?' said another. But they did not raise their voices, and the silence of the dark night remained undisturbed. Bant soon stopped feeling any pain. 'No one will come to save you,' said an assailant and they drove away into the darkness.

Bant Singh recalled later, 'I remained conscious all through and, after the first few blows, I had stopped feeling the physical pain. I don't know why I did not fall unconscious. Was it the hard will of a labourer or was it the blessing of my grandfather Dhanna Singh which kept me conscious? The only thoughts which came to my mind were of my children. What would become of them? The bag with the khoya, which was lost, the sweets that were to be made from the khoya, the Lohri bonfire; nothing came to my mind. I did not even think of Dulla Bhatti. I thought of Harbans telling me not to venture out but there was nothing that I could do to let her know of what had happened. I thought of my children; little Paroche, who slept on my arm, as I lay there under the open sky waiting for no one.'

Before and After

Even your dust is soothing, like kohl to the eyes,
O road leading to the home of my beloved

—Sohan Singh Misha

HARBANS KEPT LOOKING at Bant cycling away and prayed to the Wahe Guru to look after this man, the bread-winner of the family, the father of their eight children.

She had fallen in love with him when her bua had allowed her a glance at the man she was to marry and the love had not faded even by a shade in the rough and tumble of their life. She recalled him as he was—slim and dark, with sparkling eyes and a winsome smile. She even remembered the pink turban he was wearing that day and his crisp white shirt. When he had come to their home the first day, she had brought a tumbler full of lassi to him and their fingers had touched. Harbans blushed to think how every pore of her body had tingled. That was also the day when she had heard him sing for the first time. It was a song by Udasi, and if her body had tingled at his touch, his rich voice rising in song had stirred her soul.

The day's chores done, she lay down on the cot, still looking at the road. She had been luckier than her friends and cousins because she had found a good man who cared for her and the children. He was different from all the others.

~

The Ballad of Bant Singh

Bant's story could never be complete without his songs, which have always given him strength to strive for a better tomorrow and to live with pride even when much is lost. A song sung by Sant Ram Udasi that he heard as a boy in his goatherd days was to decide the course of Bant's life. 'The day would be spent with the goats but the evenings were free. After the evening meal we would sit listening to the stories our elders told us. Sometimes one of our uncles would play the radio and we would all gather round it,' says Bant.

He recalled that one evening there was much excitement in the village. A political rally was to be held in the compound of the village school. Many said that Sant Ram Udasi would be coming to sing at the rally. Bant did not know of him but he eagerly attended the rally. There were speeches that ten-year-old Bant could not quite understand and he wondered when the songs would begin. When he saw a lean man with a squint, wearing a shirt, trousers and a black turban, climb on to the stage, he was disappointed. He nudged his grandfather. 'Is he Sant Ram Udasi?'

'Yes, he is.'

'How will this marhchu sing? He is much too thin,' Bant said dismissively, accustomed as he was to the strapping frames of his relatives as well as the muscular, well-built landlords.

'Now you stop your chatter,' Dhanna Singh scolded,

'and let me listen. I haven't come here to hear you babble. It would be good if you listened too.'

And wasn't it excellent! Udasi's voice came deep from within his chest as he began his song, his right hand on his ear and his left raised to the audience with his eyes closed, as if in deep meditation. When the notes of the song echoed, Bant felt his whole body and soul responding, as though music was entering every pore. Everyone listened mesmerized, for it was not just the magic of music but the lyrics of the song which were sending messages of hope and struggle. Bant still remembered the song:

> Desh hai piara sanu zindagi piari nalon
> Desh ton piare ihade lok haniya
> Asee todh deni lahu wali jok haniya
>
> Our country is dearer to us than our own lives
> The people are dearer even than the country, my friend
> We will put an end to the blood-sucking leeches, my friend.

The lyrics and the tune went straight to Bant's heart. It was a song about his own life. He loved the lovelorn, plaintive notes of his grandfather's songs, but Udasi's took him to another world—a world without oppression, where everyone would have enough to eat and live with dignity. The song had actually opened the windows of his mind so that he could truly understand the speeches which followed, calling out to the workers to rise and battle for their rights. 'For weeks I sang Udasi's song. It was like each word and note was recorded in my mind. After that I made it a point to attend every rally in the neighbouring villages where Udasi would sing. I was free in the evenings and these rallies were held after the workers had done their day's work and had eaten their evening meal. Sometimes I walked many miles with my cousins just to hear Udasi's songs.'

The songs of Udasi became a source of informal education and, in a way, the school that he had never attended. One by one, they became a part of Bant's memory. 'I learnt that Udasi was related to us. His sister was married to my sister's brother-in-law in Aklia village. I was thrilled when I got a chance to meet him. He was a school teacher and he always wore a shirt and trousers. In winter he wore a coat. In the day time he would wear dark glasses, which concealed his squint,' recalled Bant, who had learnt by that time that you do not have to be stout and hefty to sing well—poetry and music have everything to do with the spirit of a person. A high point in Bant's life came when he sang Udasi's song in the poet's presence. 'I don't know if I sang well, but Udasi really encouraged me. The first time that he asked me to sing at a Party rally, I was only twelve. After that I would sing at every rally I went to. He told me that I would go very far because the quality of my voice was very good.'

Before and After

A pilgrimage in Bant's youth was a visit to Udasi's village, Raisar. 'He was not at home and I was told that I would find him by the village pond. There he was by the beautiful village pond sitting under a banyan tree and writing a poem in his diary.'

The pond was Udasi's favourite spot and from his youth onwards he would lead the buffaloes to it, a notebook in his pocket. While the buffaloes cooled themselves in the water, the poet, who was also born into a family of Mazhabi Sikhs, would sit beneath the old banyan tree and pen his poems. His poetry was guided by the calm environment of his village and his own struggle amidst want and poverty. Of all the Punjabi poets who were inspired by the Naxalite movement in Punjab, Udasi truly remains a people's poet.

~

The pond at Raisar was still as beautiful as Bant remembered it to be some three decades ago, with old banyan trees at its edge. My guide on this poetic pilgrimage was not Bant but Rajinder Rahi, who is also an ardent admirer of Udasi. Rahi took upon himself the task of editing and publishing the poetry, life sketches and interviews of the poet.

The drive from Rahi's village, Chak Bhaika, in Ludhiana district to Raisar in Barnala district took twenty minutes. This is a rather remote and untouched

The Ballad of Bant Singh

area of Malwa, and picturesque, with old trees, gushing irrigation canals and glimpses of the white domes of gurudwaras in the distance; the narrow winding road itself was shaded by trees. This was also the area which saw intense activity during the few years of the Naxalite uprising and the long years of the militant movement when separatists struggled for the imagined Sikh state of Khalistan. But we were not talking of all that then, it was poetry time. Poetry and music were an integral part of the journeys I made to gather Bant's ballad. That was how it had to be.

Remarking on the beauty of the road, Rahi started reciting lines from a poem by another fine and almost forgotten poet of Punjabi, Sohan Singh Misha:

> Teri dhoorh vi surme vargi
> Mittran de ghar jandiye sadhke
>
> Even your dust is soothing, like kohl to the eyes,
> O road leading to the home of my beloved.

Udasi was truly beloved by hundreds and rarely did a poet enjoy such admiration, from the working class and the intellectuals alike, as he did. He rose from poverty and stigma to become a people's poet. But the trials and tribulations he faced through his life led to alcohol addiction and a disturbed mind, and Udasi died an anonymous death on the upper berth of a train compartment. His family, waiting for him in Raisar, merely received a telegram: 'Sant Ram Udasi found expired at Manmad railway station.' But he left behind a legacy of songs which will stir even a stone. No meet of Punjabi activists, be it in Bathinda or Birmingham, is complete without an Udasi song. If the singer were to forget a line, sure enough, someone from the audience will get up and sing it.

There we were at the pond where Bant had gone to look for Udasi. It was evening and the still water was shadowed by the ancient banyan trees which stood by its banks. A folk song in Punjabi says that trees may be mute but they know well all human sorrows. These trees had been witness to the sorrows of Udasi who struggled hard for social justice but who had to face the humiliations of poverty, class and caste all through his life only to find himself alone, persecuted and alcoholic, and who died at the early age of forty-seven.

From the village we went to Barnala to meet Udasi's second daughter Pritpal. A pharmacist in the civil hospital, she recalled the latter years of Udasi when, instead of going to the pond, he would sit in the village gurudwara and write his poems. 'We three daughters were very precious to him. He educated us in grave economic want and in the face of opposition from the family. I wish he had lived to see us standing on our own feet,' she said. Both Rahi and Pritpal were anxious because their application to the Punjab government to name the school in Raisar after Udasi had been pending for the last five years. The Jats of the village were trying to thwart that move by demanding that the school be named after a Jat army officer who was killed in action. This is how Dalit histories are excluded surely but steadily. But, eventually, the admirers of Udasi won the battle and the school now bears the name of the poet of the village who taught hundreds of students their mother tongue.

The poet was born midst abject poverty to Mehar Singh and Dhan Kaur, who were followers of the Udasi sect, a celibate order of yogis which was founded by Baba Siri Chand, the eldest son of Guru Nanak. A weak and sickly baby, Udasi developed an eye infection when still a child. His parents took him to the dera of Sadhu Ishar Das in the village of Mome near Raisar and prayed that his eyes should not deteriorate further. Dhan Kaur pledged that if his eyes became all right she would gift her son to the dera where he would serve as a sadhu.

With time and treatment, his eyes did get better and, true to her word, Dhan Kaur took Udasi to the dera and put him in the sadhu's lap saying: 'I had pledged that if his eyes get better I will give him to the dera to work and serve as a sadhu.'

The sadhu blessed the boy and said with foresight, 'I accept your offering but I do not want you to make him a sadhu. Send him to school, educate him, and one day

Before and After

he will shine like a star.' This is how Udasi's education began. He showed academic promise and a talent for music and theatre. His early poems were influenced by the valour and sacrifice of Sikh saints. His transition to revolutionary poetry came with the ultra-Left wave in Punjab. This was his most productive period as a poet, and also the most tumultous as he was constantly in flight, thrown out of his job as a government school teacher and subjected to violent torture by the police. The abuse was far more frequent and severe where people from the lower castes were concerned, especially those who dared to participate in movements calling for an equal society. Dalit poet Lal Singh Dil, who came into prominence with the Naxalite movement, recounts the caste bias which accompanied the humiliating third-degree torture in his autobiography *Dastaan*: 'I heard the familiar words from the mouth of a new policeman, "So you bloody Chamars, you want our land?"'

Bant was just a toddler when Punjab saw its flash of spring thunder, after Dil recited his poem *Sham da Rang* (Evening Tide)—describing a caravan of landless labourers moving from one destination to another—and radical thinkers declared that revolution was at hand. Both Dil and Udasi became representative poets of the times in different ways, but their strength came from the fact that theirs was a lived experience of oppression and poverty. Dil, with his abstraction and blank verse, was the poets' poet and Udasi, with his songs, reached straight into the hearts of the working class—or, should we say, the working caste.

It was exposure to Udasi's songs and workers' meetings which drew Bant to the Communist Party of India (Marxist-Leninist) (CPI-ML). In a few years he became an active member of the Naujawan Bharat Sabha, formed by Bhagat Singh and his comrades in 1926 and revived in Punjab in 1970 during the Naxalite movment. Later he joined the Indian People's Front and also had a brief stint with the Bahujan Samaj Party. 'That I did in anger because the candidate of our Party who was elected as MLA seemed to have lost all contact with the workers,' he recalls of the last with a chuckle. However, it was in the Mazdoor Mukti Morcha that Bant truly discovered his abilities as a leader and started enlisting and organizing labourers.

His political activities apart, the adolescent Bant knew that his goatherding days would soon be at an end and he was looking for a way to earn a livelihood without having to work in the fields which belonged to the Jat landlords. Bant started earning his living by selling vegetables. His older brother, Ajmer Singh, had already started his own little business of buying cosmetics from nearby towns and selling them in rural fairs. 'I was very attached to this brother of mine. He married a girl from Maur Mandi and my bhabhi Ranjit Kaur was a very beautiful woman. She came from town so she carried herself better and wore well-matched clothes. I just could not take my eyes off her as she moved around the house in a bright suit, glass bangles tinkling on her wrists as she did the household chores. I can never forget the marriage and my first trip to Maur Mandi,' said Bant.

During his childhood, the high point of the wedding season would be the feast, with dishes of pumpkin and potatoes. 'In those days vegetables were not easily available in villages and eating pumpkin or potatoes was a big thing,' he said, and then interrupted the conversation to tell his daughter Sukhminder to cook pumpkin for the evening meal. The green pumpkin had been sent by his daughter Baljit who lives with her husband Resham and three children in a village near Sirsa. On this visit, I was staying for dinner so he insisted that the meal should include something sweet, too. So milk and rice were put on the stove for kheer and Bant sent his son Manjit to the village shop for some raisins, almonds and dried coconut. Brass bowls full of delicious kheer were served before the meal. A little while later, pumpkin mash, laced with desi ghee, was served with fresh chapatis, also smeared with ghee. 'Put a piece of pickle on the thali,' Bant instructed and a piece of mango pickled with fennel seeds in the typical Punjabi style was given to me. This was one among the many fine meals I ate in his home.

The Ballad of Bant Singh

The Mazhabi Sikhs eat well and have a hospitable disposition. Rahi, who is one of the better off among the Mazhabis, being the owner of four acres of land, says, 'The people of my community are large-hearted, unlike many other castes. The poorest of the poor will spend what they have and most of what they earn goes into food as there is no reaching for more acquisitions on the meagre earnings of hard labour. What is praiseworthy is that they will share it with others.' The poet Udasi's daughter, Iqbal, a village school principal, in childhood memories of her father recalls him returning home 'with two kilos of grapes and a kilo of meat'.

But happy as these recollections are, the darker side of village life can never be suppressed. Bant's brother and sister-in-law had a daughter named Pammy and a son named Soma. Bant loved playing with them when they were young. A proud uncle, he recounted: 'My nephew has an electric goods shop and my niece is married.' He is happy that the children have done well in spite of the tragedy that shattered their lives. This—which left its mark on Bant's young mind—was the death of his brother, who committed suicide by swallowing pesticide. It arose, according to Bant, from a minor domestic quarrel with his wife. 'Had he just waited for a few hours and let his mind cool down, this would never have happened,' he said with regret. Sadly, ingesting pesticide is the most common way of committing suicide in rural Punjab because of its easy availability. Suicides are an increasingly common phenomenon, not only among Jat farmers but among agricultural labourers, too. The latter, however, do not make news. Farmers are under pressure because of the bank loans they have taken, and which they find themselves unable to repay; the labourers are equally desperate because of the—usually much smaller—loans they have taken from Jat farmers to meet wedding or illness expenses. Both categories are severely indebted and many among them seek the same terrible way out.

Bant, who was then selling vegetables, decided to follow his late brother's trade of selling cosmetics and trinkets at village melas. Punjab has fairs and festivals aplenty and they still attract thousands in the rural areas. Besides the famous Baisakhi mela of Damdama Sahib, Hola Mohalla of Anandpur Sahib and the Maghi mela of Muktsar, there are hundreds of smaller melas from village to village and shrine to shrine. 'I decided to peddle cosmetics because the work was less messy than selling vegetables and it also meant more money. My bhabhi's relatives in Maur Mandi put me in touch with wholesale merchants,' said Bant and added with a laugh, 'soon I knew all there was to know about powder and surkhian (lipsticks)!'

In fact it was the business of cosmetics that brought Bant and Harbans together. Melas meant brisk business but, instead of just waiting for them, Bant started selling door-to-door too. His cheerful disposition and his way with words made him a good salesman. 'This is what led to my marriage with Harbans Kaur,' confided Bant. Harbans, sitting by his side, nodded her head, blushing like a young girl.

'Did he come to your house to sell you powder and lipsticks?' I asked.

'Oh no! Nothing of the kind,' she said, laughing, and covering her face with her hands.

'How did you meet then?'

Bant replied, 'We never met before our marriage. See, I married her without even setting my eyes on her.'

'Well, so did she,' I said, taking her side. I turned to Harbans. 'Did you come to know well beforehand that you were going to marry a very smart and handsome man?'

'I had just got a glance of him in my bua's home', Harbans said, looking fondly at her husband. Clearly, that first glance had been so magical that she was still in love.

'You know what happened?' Bant intervened, picking up the threads of the story of their coming together, 'I would often go to my ancestral Aklia village for door-to-door sales. There are some two hundred and fifty Dalit homes in Aklia and many of our relatives are there. I was in her aunt's house showing cosmetics. Her aunt and uncle got into a conversation with me.'

Before and After

'How much do you earn?' her uncle asked Bant.

'I manage to make a hundred a day, and more during melas.'

This was enough for the girl's family to make up their minds. 'Those were times when daily wages for a farm labourer would be only fifteen or, at the most, twenty rupees. So in comparison I was a prince,' Bant told me.

In a few days, the family was at Bant's home in Burj Jhabbar making the offer of marriage for their daughter to Bant's parents. Jagir Singh and Bachan Kaur happily accepted. They too were keen to see their youngest child married so, in a few months, the wedding took place. Bant was just eighteen and Harbans a couple of years older—such differences in age do not matter much in rural areas. Harbans was the eldest daughter of a Mazhabi family in Kaleke village near Dhaula in Sangrur district. 'I had two older brothers and four sisters and a brother younger than me. We were a family of eight. My mother was often ill and I looked after the children and did the chores at home. I saw very hard times from the beginning,' said Harbans.

This perhaps was the happiest moment in the toil and trouble of her life, and the two were married in the first month of 1984. Those were turbulent times. Militancy was at its peak in Punjab with the Sikh separatist leader Jarnail Singh Bhindranwale presiding over an armed movement for the creation of the Sikh state of Khalistan. That year saw the unfortunate Operation Bluestar in which the Indian Army stormed the Golden Temple to flush out the militants and many, including Bhindranwale, were killed. Many innocent pilgrims, too, lost their lives. Sikh sentiments were deeply outraged and later that year two Sikh bodyguards of Prime Minister Indira Gandhi assassinated her. In a bizarre backlash, innocent Sikhs were killed all over the country. Militancy grew stronger in Punjab with some of the Naxalites too turning Khalistani. The movement had considerable support from the people and more so in rural areas because the Sikhs felt that they had been wronged. This continued until the movement deteriorated and started losing popular support in rural areas. It was finally crushed by the state.

The Khalistani movement was led by Jat Sikhs but included many Dalits in its cadre. Rahi, who is persona non grata as far as the Leftists in Punjab go, as his Khalistani leanings are widely suspected, said: 'Many Naxalites from our area joined the Khalistani movement and there were Dalits among them. However, all the Khalistanis from these parts were aware activists and none of them stooped to killing innocent people as was happening those days.' Perhaps he had forgotten the killings of innocent migrant labourers working in mills in Barnala and surrounding areas. He also narrated that

Before and After

Udasi—a pillar of the Naxalite uprising and its bard, too—underwent an ideological shift in favour of a separate state for the Sikhs. According to Rahi, the killing of the Sikhs in 1984 disturbed Udasi and, in an interview taped by Rahi and three other comrades, the poet said that while the Naxalite uprising was just an action, the Khalistani wave was a real peasants' movement in revolt against the oppression of the Sikhs by the state. When asked to comment on the killing of his close friend and comrade, Baldev Singh Maan, Udasi was reported to have said that every movement had wrong elements and this was a deed committed by some misled brothers. However, many deny that such an interview took place. Udasi is not around anymore to confirm or to deny his statement, but the Leftists in Punjab do not want to believe this of their beloved poet. As for Bant, he had turned nineteen in 1984 and was an active member of the Indian People's Front. 'I was never a part of the Khalistani movement and not sympathetic to it either. My stand was that of my Party: the killing of innocent people was wrong, either by the militants or by the police. Punjabis were killing Punjabis and that was something sorrowful,' he said.

~

Bant enjoyed talking about his wedding. Knowing his interest in good food, I asked Bant whether a goat was slaughtered on that occasion. He replied, 'Yes, we slaughtered a goat because my sister and I were married at the same time. I was married just one day later. The same happened with Harbans. She was married a day before her younger brother.'

This is the norm in most Dalit families and the principal reason for this is to save expense. The second reason is that the household work passes on from the sister to the sister-in-law. 'Now that Sukhminder's marriage is settled we are looking for a good girl for my eldest son Nirbhay so that his wife can come and take over all the chores that our daughter does,' Bant said. In a Dalit household everyone has to work, either in the fields or at home.

Meanwhile, Hardeep brought forth a framed photograph—tinted rather gaudily—of the bride and the groom with her parents. The couple looked radiant, especially Harbans. There was a shy smile on her moon-shaped face.

'Just look at my face. I was as round as you are,' she said to me, adding, 'worry and illness have left me frail.'

'What was the colour of your wedding suit?'

Before she could answer, Bant replied, 'It was magenta. The photographer has not got the colour right in this picture. See, she is wearing the suit I gave her and I am wearing the sky-blue check shirt with a turban to match and dark blue pants, which her family gave me.'

Before and After

He went on, 'Along with the suit, I sent her cosmetics. In fact I sent her two boxes of powders, two lipsticks, two nail varnishes and two bottles of scent. I was giving her a choice that if she did not like one, she could use the other.' Also, Bant set about the task of building a room for himself and his wife in his parental house, as is done—if space is available—by every Dalit boy who is about to get married. In other cases, a room is vacated by the elders who move out to the courtyard. 'Those were days when bricks were far cheaper than today. Still, I spent a princely sum of two thousand eight hundred rupees to buy eight thousand bricks that went into building our room. Much later I added another small room.'

Harbans's brothers did their best to give her a good send-off. In rural Punjab of yore it was customary for Jats to plant a tahli (shisham) tree when a girl was born and, by the time she was sixteen, it would yield the wood required for the pieces of furniture for the trousseau. One would be a tall and wide box called a peti that would hold the girl's bedding, clothes and utensils. It would be decorated with tiles, mirrors, brass knobs and carvings. The other would be the bridal bed with a mirror fitted into the backrest to serve as a dresser. Harbans's family were poor agrarian labourers and had no fields and no shisham trees but one of her older brothers was employed by the Forest Department to fell trees when required. He managed to get some wood and there was major excitement when he took upon himself the task of fashioning a box and a bed for his much-loved sister who had shouldered the responsibilities of her parental home so well. Harbans still has the box and she uses it to store their winter clothes and bedding. It is nailed with strips of wood on which are carved leaves. The front of the box has cutouts with glass-framed pictures of the Sikh Gurus and Bhagat Singh. With these gifts of good luck, Harbans moved into Bant's mud-and-brick home and the young couple began a relationship of mutual care and concern that is still going strong. 'We saw good times and we saw bad times but we were always together in sharing joy and sorrows,' said Harbans.

Sorrow came first when the couple lost their firstborn son when he was only four days old. 'We had been really happy when the child was born but he went away too soon. I coped with the loss but Harbans took it very badly. She would just lie in bed with her face to the wall and hardly speak,' recalled Bant.

'For nine months I had cherished hope in my womb but I got only four days with the baby. My breasts were overflowing with milk but there was no one to drink it,' rued Harbans.

Bant decided that the best way to draw her out of depression was to get her busy with work. He started taking her with him as he sold cosmetics door-to-door. This proved to be a great healer. Harbans would dress up every morning and go out with Bant, sitting on the crossbar of his bicycle. She would then meet women and talk to them. This helped her to overcome her sorrow and she was soon her old self. Bant also saw that the women were more comfortable dealing with Harbans so he handed over the responsibility of door-to-door sales to her and kept the job of setting up stalls at fairs and festivals for himself.

Then Harbans conceived a second time and was very apprehensive about the outcome. But this time good fortune was smiling and a baby girl was born. 'People usually don't celebrate the birth of a girl but he was overjoyed,' she recounted.

Bant was so thrilled to be father to a daughter that he cycled to Joga and brought back laddoos and patasas. He went to every home in the vehra distributing the sweets.

'Look at him! My boy has gone mad,' exclaimed his mother, Bachan Kaur.

The neighbours were surprised too. Some old woman chided him, 'Bant, you crazy boy, what are you doing? Who distributes sweets at the birth of a daughter!'

'I do.' Bant laughed, and said, 'She is more than a son to us.'

Recounting the joys of that day, Bant started humming lines from one of his favourite Udasi songs:

The Ballad of Bant Singh

Dhian jammdian te gurh vi nahi mangade
Mera ki kasoor, Babula?

They don't even ask for jaggery at the birth of a girl
What is my fault, Father?

Bant truly believes in what he sings and so this new father rejected the idea of a girl's birth being an unhappy event by distributing the sweets considered most auspicious by Punjabis. This is what sets Bant apart as a singer. For him, a song is not just for song's sake, it stands for social and political change.

Bant found a name for the newborn from the scriptures of the Sikh Gurus, a practice that he repeated for his eight children, and the baby was named Baljit. The name means 'the strength to win' and that is how Bant wanted to see his daughter: a winner always.

The Long Road to Mansa

We bore the blows of sticks on our bodies in the streets
But we never let our rights shiver in the cold!

—Udasi

HARBANS GOT UP from the cot and stretched herself. There was no end to recalling the joys and sorrows of life. Night was approaching and she must get the evening meal ready; Bant would soon be returning. It was cold and the children were huddled in the room. Sukhminder was lighting the stove. Dinner was to be potatoes in gravy and rotis. Harbans thought that when Bant returned she would quickly scramble some eggs to make a bhurji; he usually liked something savoury with his evening drink.

Soon it was evening but there was no sign of the man of the house. The children were hungry so Harbans asked them to eat and started feeding the youngest one.

'When will Bhapa come?' the young one wanted to know.

'He should be here soon. He said he would return before dark. Maybe he has stopped in the village to meet someone,' she replied, and turned to Sukhminder. 'Listen, girl, you eat. I will wait for your Bhapa. Just put our roti-sabzi by the side. I will warm it up when he comes.'

Dinner over, the girls cuddled up under one quilt

and the boys under another. Paroche started whimpering as his mother tried to put him to bed: 'I will sleep on Bhapa's arm. I always do.'

Harbans patted him and said: 'Tonight you sleep on my arm and when Bhapa comes I will turn you over to him. You know he has gone to Dhilwan to get khoya so that I can make you tasty sweets for Lohri.'

'I will eat both gajar halwa and pinni,' Paroche declared. All the others laughed, not knowing that it would be a long time before they would all laugh together again.

All the children were asleep but for the eldest, Nirbhay. The night was thickening and fog was enveloping the village. Harbans started feeling uneasy and sent Nirbhay to his uncle's house to find out if there was any news about his father, but Nirbhay returned saying that no message had come so far. Harbans felt her left eye flutter—this was not a good sign. Then she scolded herself, thinking that Bant always dismissed such omens, saying, 'You are a Comrade's wife, you cannot believe in such mumbo-jumbo.' A smile came to her lips and she too drifted off to sleep, only to be woken by a loud knocking on the door.

Harbans got up to open the door, thankful that Bant was home at last. But it wasn't Bant at the door but Hansa, his brother. Harbans stared at him in fear; what tidings had he brought? 'I just got a call on the mobile

The Long Road to Mansa

from Beant Akali. Bant was beaten up and thrown in the fields. Beant has taken him to the Mansa hospital. Don't worry, all will be well. Just get ready and we will leave for Mansa at day break. You catch a little sleep now.'

But sleep eluded Harbans. She sat stunned, as though she had turned into stone and could return to human form only with the first rays of sun in the wintery sky.

~

Despite his awful injuries, Bant fought to remain conscious. He waited for no one but providence itself seemed to be waiting on him. Beant Akali, who had met him as he stood musing by the fields in the afternoon, was sitting in a friend's automobile spare parts shop in Joga. 'Every evening a few of us would gather at the shop to drink a cup of hot tea and sometimes something more spirited. I was there as I had gone to Mansa and had stopped for a chit-chat,' Beant recalled, as he told me the story of the rescue and the ride through the dark night to the hospital in Mansa. Bant and Beant's friendship went back many years, even though they had little in common by way of caste or class or, for that matter, political ideology.

Beant Singh was a proud member of the Akali Dal. Most other Jats of the village owed allegiance to the Congress. The politics of the state, with all its permutations and combinations, permeates right down to the remotest village through the supporters of rival political groups, and so it was with Burj Jhabbar. When Beant won the elections for the post of sarpanch in the village, the Congress-backed landlords who had held this post in turn for several decades could not dream of letting their powerful citadel go and, with it, all the privileges they enjoyed at the grassroots. They swore that Beant would not remain sarpanch. A writ was filed in court challenging the result on the basis of unfair practices and there it languished till the term ended. The Akali was just not allowed to function as a sarpanch. Aspersions were cast that Bant had played a role in taking away a chunk of the Mazhabi votes to tilt the balance in favour of the Akali. Beant responded with bravado, but those who had held power for so long proved too clever for him. Thus the two namesakes were united in their differences with the power-brokers of Burj Jhabbar.

It fell to Beant's lot to look for Bant in the fields and take him to hospital on that unhappy night. Beant has told this story many times over, yet he never tires of it. He describes his experience down to the last detail and with much enthusiasm, never failing to take the credit for saving a 'poor' man's life. In spite of their bond, and the difference of just one letter of the alphabet in their names, the caste-class difference between the saviour and the victim remains, and Beant incessantly used the phrase, 'a poor man'.

'I was at the spare-parts shop in Joga with friends. It was very cold so we were drinking some hot tea and eating samosas brought from the halwai across the road. The samosas were good but there was too much sugar in the tea. But at least it was keeping us warm. Just then my mobile rang. I wondered who was calling—I thought it must be my wife wanting to know when I would be home.' But from the other end came the scared voice of a boy. 'As the boy spoke, his words slurred. At first I thought it was some drunken fellow playing a prank. I asked who was speaking and he said he was Appy, son of Amrik Singh. This alerted me because Amrik Singh owned the ration store which had lost its licence after Bant and his Party had campaigned against hoarding and other irregularities.' The boy went on to say, 'We beat up your man and he is lying half-dead in the fields. Go and save him if you so desire.' The Akali was surprised by this strange message. 'If they wanted to kill someone, why were they asking me to go and save him? I told my friends and their first reaction was that a trap was being laid for me. I was being called to a deserted spot only to be attacked. Otherwise, why should a culprit show off his crime in so strange a manner? It was only later that the reason became clear: if Bant was to die in the fields, the offence would be greater in the eyes of the law.'

The Ballad of Bant Singh

The Akali was undecided about what he should do. He conferred with his friends but all of them advised him not to get mixed up in the matter. One said, 'The telephone has come from youths supported by the Congress, Bant is a Communist, why should an Akali like you intervene?' Disturbed by the message, Beant said, 'I gulped down the over-sweetened tea and, bidding my friends adieu, got up to return home.' However, he confessed, he kept thinking of the boy's slurred words and the feeling of unease did not leave him. The information given to him on the telephone could be a lie, but what if it was true?

Finally the voice of his conscience triumphed and he told his wife Gurmeet Kaur that he had decided to take a chance and look for the man left half-dead in the fields. Something told him that he must.

'If you can save a poor man's life then why not do it? I know you will not be at peace unless you make an effort. But do take your gun with you for safety,' Gurmeet told her husband.

Carrying his gun and taking two farmhands along, Beant set out in his Maruti to the Dhilwan link road. If a life could be saved, they would do their utmost save it. It was dark and quiet and fog had settled in a thick blanket. Nevertheless, the three of them raced through the fields looking for Bant, but he was not to be found. They looked around for over an hour, but there was no sign of him.

The Long Road to Mansa

Bant, who had been lying in the fields for several hours by then, heard some voices and thought that the boys had come back to finish him off. He called out, 'Come and kill me or take me to hospital.' Hearing his voice pierce the still darkness, the rescuers ran towards him. One of the farmhands who reached first was so horrified at the state Bant was in that he fainted. When Beant reached the spot, Bant said: 'First take care of this man and then attend to me.'

'The first thing I did was place my hand on Bant's forehead and, to my horror, I found it stone cold. I had a woolen muffler wrapped round my head. I took it off and wrapped it round his head. Next I wondered how we would pick him up and put him into the car. I tried to raise his arm and it folded like the sleeve of a cotton shirt. I tried to lift his leg and it was the same.'

Finally, the blanket which one of the farmhands had draped over himself was spread out and the three of them somehow lifted Bant by his torso and put him on the blanket. They caught hold of the ends of the blanket and carried him to the car. 'We had made this much progress, but I was not sure that he would survive the thirty-five-kilometre journey to the Mansa Civil Hospital because his condition was so bad. I folded my hands seeking Wahe Guru's blessings and started the car,' Beant Singh related, his photographic memory recalling every detail of that terrible night.

The Ballad of Bant Singh

Beant started driving faster than he had ever done with the grace of Wahe Guru's blessings. Every fraction of a second seemed precious and he was plagued by the thought that he was losing time even in stopping to get petrol. The hurdles seemed to be endless—a ditch here, a shadow there, a truck which would not let them overtake. And when they approached the railway crossing, the barrier came down.

'Now Mansa was just twenty-five kilometres away but it seemed to be twenty-five thousand kilometres away. I put my hand out, lifted the barrier and drove past. A police patrol jeep parked there started chasing us and thus we reached the hospital, with a jeep full of cops following us.'

The policemen rushed out to accost Beant for breaking traffic rules by crossing the barrier in so cavalier a manner.

'I told them, arrest me if you must or challan me, but I was just trying to save a poor man's life.'

What amazed the Akali was that Bant remained conscious right through and, during the race to Mansa, told him the entire story of the assault on him and even gave him the names of the youths who attacked had him. The names were Sandeep, Honey, Appy, Gurditta, Didar, Bikky and Babli. These were common enough names and nicknames—every neighbourhood in Punjab has dozens of boys with such names—but their act was anything but neighbourly.

The Long Road to Mansa

One would have thought that things would get better once they reached the hospital, but this was not to be. Bant was put on to a stretcher and wheeled into the hospital foyer and a new phase of trials began. There was nothing civil about the Mansa Civil Hospital. First, the hospital staff was reluctant to admit the grievously injured man as it was a medico-legal case and that required the police to record a statement. Once that was accomplished, there was no one to attend to him.

When Beant went to the doctor on duty pleading that Bant be moved to the Emergency ward, the doctor chose to turn a deaf ear. When he persisted, the doctor put forward a most indecent and unethical proposal.

'I was shocked when this doctor, named Parshotam Goel, laughed and said that I knew what I needed to do if I wanted the patient to be moved to the Emergency ward,' Beant recounted.

'What do you want me to do? I am just trying to save the poor man's life.'

'What will I get out of it?'

The doctor said that since the patient was poor he would take a bribe of just a thousand rupees. Beant had started from home with twelve hundred rupees in his pocket but had spent eight hundred on petrol. How could the deficit of six hundred rupees be arranged at that hour of the night? However, he ran to the chemist's shop outside to see if he could borrow money. Although the chemist was willing to lend him some, he had already sent the cash-box home, which was a long distance away. Not just that, the boy who had taken the cash-box did not have a mobile phone so there was no means of calling him back. However, the chemist readily lent the three hundred rupees that he had in his own pocket.

'Sometimes help comes from the most unexpected quarters,' said Beant. 'The tea-vendor, who was witnessing my predicament, came forward and offered the much-needed three hundred rupees. I thanked him and assured him that the money would be returned to him the next day.' The tea-vendor was a man called Pappey, who had know Bant for several years. Whenever the latter brought someone to the hospital for a check-up, he made it a point to ask after Pappey's welfare, have a cup of tea with him, and once in a while even sing a song as he sat there.

'Do not worry about the money, make haste and get treatment for the patient,' was Pappey's reply.

The Akali did so but he could not help contrasting the inhumane doctor with the compassionate tea-vendor. Justice came much later when, after sustained protests by the Mazdoor Mukti Morcha, the doctor was suspended from service for his disgraceful act.

That cruel night of 5 January somehow passed and the following morning news got around and Bant's family, Party colleagues and relatives reached the hospital. Hope for Bant's survival was slim. His wife said, 'I was too dazed to react. I had seen many sorrows in my life but this was the worst of all. What was to become of us all?'

Baljit and her husband reached at mid-day. Even today Baljit's eyes flash with anger when she describes her feelings on seeing her dear father in such a miserable state. The younger children were not told how serious their father's condition was. But instinct seemed to tell them that this Lohri there would be no bonfire, no sweets and no singing of the song of Dulla Bhatti. Young Hardeep suddenly seemed to understand how the zamindars took away the humble sweets of the labourers and what the 'loot' of the landlords was all about.

The Colour Violet

My mother, do not give us birth in a village
Where dreams remain forever shackled

—Udasi

AS BALJIT WENT about her morning chores she hummed this poignant song by Udasi, a girl's request that she be born elsewhere. Her hand went to her stomach. A new sapling had been planted in her womb and she had a feeling that her second-born would be a girl—a girl who would have a life very different from her mother's. Baljit was a determined soul and she told herself that she would make sure that her daughter should have a better life. Musing thus she put the pot on for the morning tea. Just then, she heard her husband Resham's mobile phone ring. Her heart skipped a beat. Who could be calling so early? Pouring tea into glass tumblers, she went into the room. Resham was sitting underneath a quilt and his brow was wrinkled.

Handing him a glass, Baljit asked: 'What is the matter? Who was calling so early in the morning?'

'Oh, nothing. It was my friend Kartara. He wanted to know if I could take him to the fields on my bicycle. His tyre is punctured.'

'All right, I got worried for a moment,' Baljit said, sipping the hot and sweet milky brew.

It was not until she had fed and dressed their little

son and eaten the morning meal that the gentle and considerate Resham broke the news to her.

'Baljit, get ready. I will not go to work today. We have to go to Mansa.'

'Why, what is wrong? You told me that you were taking Kartara to the fields with you.'

'I wanted you to eat something before I gave you the bad news. Your Bhapa was attacked last night outside your village and is in the hospital at Mansa. Your uncle had called up to say that we should reach there. Your mother must have already reached.'

Baljit hurriedly got her little son ready and somehow changed her clothes. They were out in less than half an hour. The journey, with Resham by her side and her son in her arms, seemed endless. They first took a tempo to Sirsa and then a bus. Baljit was in a daze, fearing the worst, and Resham put his arm round her shoulders as the bus moved on. Feeling the warmth of his arm her thoughts turned to her father, the first man in her life whom she had loved dearly and who had returned her love in equal measure. She tried to take her mind off the present and seek refuge in reveries of her happy childhood.

~

'Bhapaji, are you taking me with you to the mela tomorrow?' the five-year-old Baljit asked Bant as she lay

The Colour Violet

by his side on a cot in the small courtyard of their old house, her head cushioned on his strong right arm.

'Yes, my dear, I am taking you to the mela tomorrow.'

'Will you take this Pammo too?' she asked, pointing to her baby sister who was being nursed on the other charpai by Harbans.

'How can I take Pammo, she is too small. She will not be able to sit on my bicycle.'

'Yes and she will do susu and keep howling at the mela,' said Baljit, wrinkling her nose with scorn—she had been making sure that the little one would not demand her father's attention on this special outing. 'And Bibi won't be there to feed Pammo,' Baljit added for good measure.

'Don't worry. I told you she is too small to go to a mela,' Bant assured his darling.

'I am not small. I am a big girl and I don't howl or do susu on everyone.'

'True dear, you are my big girl. Meri sherni!'

'And Pammo? Is she your sherni too?'

'No, she is just a little khargosh.'

'A khargosh is so small. Is a sherni big?'

'Yes, a sherni is very big.'

'Pammo is a khargosh. I am a sherni. Pammo is a...'

Harbans interrupted this father-daughter conversation. 'Rabba! This girl's tongue runs like a scissors! She's giving me a headache.'

The Ballad of Bant Singh

Bachan, Bant's mother, who was dousing the cow-dung fire in the mud stove at the other end of courtyard after the evening meal, chipped in: 'How he pampers and spoils this wretched girl. A girl should be brought up like a girl, my son, and not like a boy.'

'Bebe, give him some sense, he will not listen to me,' Harbans grumbled.

'You women will never learn anything. Children are children. So what if she is a girl? It is good for children to ask questions and one must answer them. That is how a child learns,' said Bant.

'Balle oye! Look how much she's learning. She is already competing with her baby sister. She wants all your love and attention. What will she do once she has brothers?'

There was silence and Bachan realized that she had said the wrong thing. She looked apologetically at her son and daughter-in-law. But it was too late, the words had already escaped her tongue. The silence was broken by Harbans wailing,

'Hai mere rabba! If fate had not been so cruel the girls would have had two brothers. God gave me two sons and then snatched them away. What sin had I committed that I have been punished like this?'

When Baljit was not yet two, a second son was born to them. The whole family was overjoyed. But the baby died within twenty-four hours of birth. Harbans had

The Colour Violet

not even fully recovered from the loss of her first son when this second blow came. Holding her dead child to her heart, she felt her head swim and her whole body convulsed in spasms. This was the first epileptic fit she experienced. The fits would continue to plague her for the rest of her life. In the years to come, the pain of losing her first two boys was alleviated a little by a house full of eight children—four boys and four girls. But her health was never the same again.

Bachan came to her daughter-in-law's side and said: 'Na kudiye, don't weep, don't lose heart. The Sacha Patshah is very kind. He will give you the gift of sons. It is just a question of time.'

Gradually, Harbans stopped crying. Putting Pammo by her side, she turned her tear-stained face to the sky. Bachan quietly went inside. Baljit had fallen asleep prattling on about lionesses and rabbits. Her head was still on Bant's right arm and there was a little smile on her face as she snuggled into her father's chest.

Bant told his wife, 'Look at the stars twinkling in the sky. They bring light and hope to the dark night. The dark sky of our lives is also not without hope. Just think of the two stars lying by our sides. In our sorrow, we must not forget their joys. Do not weep for that which is lost, be happy for what we have.'

The following morning Baljit was ready early. She was dressed in her best leaf-green salwar-kameez and she was her chatty self as usual: 'Bhapaji, which mela are we going to?'

'It is the mela of Jogi Pir,' Bant answered, putting a piece of the alu paraontha into her mouth.

'Who was he?'

'He was a brave man.'

'Was he braver than you?'

Bant laughed and said, 'Yes he was braver than me and also than my sherni.'

Harbans, who was frying the paraonthas stuffed with spiced and mashed potatoes, laughed, saying, 'There she goes again. Now sit down quietly and eat your paraontha. Let your father eat too. Both of you have a long day ahead.'

Baljit sat down but turning to her father pleaded lovingly, 'Bhapaji, please tell me the story of Jogi Pir.'

'Stories are told and heard only in the evenings—I have told you that before. Now, you tell me what one must do during the day.'

Baljit shut her eyes for a moment in an endearing manner and replied, 'During the day one must work.'

'True, my daughter knows everything.' Bant laughed.

Harbans, too, had woken up in a cheerful frame of mind. 'Now don't spoil her so. Baljit, remember to feed your father and you too must eat in the afternoon. I have packed paraonthas and pickle for you.'

Bant wheeled out his bicycle and hung two bags full

The Colour Violet

of cosmetics and toys from the handles. He had started selling toys too once Baljit turned a toddler and there was always a supply of plastic toys for his daughter. Baljit put her arms round her father's neck and held on to him tightly as they moved out of their home to the mela of Jogi Pir in the nearby village of Bhopal.

It was morning and people had not started pouring in yet. Picking a suitable place to set up his stall, and leaving his wares in the care of a cousin, Bant took Baljit to see the statue of Jogi Pir, an ancestor of the Chahal Jats who had bravely fought Taimur the Lame. Legend has it that even after his head was cut off, his body kept fighting on. Baljit looked in wonder at the statue of a handsome man in fine robes riding a horse and with a dog accompanying them.

'But Bhapaji, his head is there,' Baljit said.

'This is a statue but, you know, fairies brought back his head from the battle field.'

'Fairies?'

'The Chahal women were so beautiful that they were called fairies.'

'Bhapaji, will you tell me the story of these fairies tonight?'

'We will see that when night comes. Now, you enjoy the day. You know, they say if you fold your hands and ask for something, Jogi Pir grants your wish.'

'What should I wish for?'

'It is your choice.'

Baljit shut her eyes for a moment and said: 'I will ask for brothers so that Bibi will not weep.'

~

My meeting with Baljit came many months after I started visiting Bant's village to interview him and others around him. Now a mother of three children, Baljit smiled as she recalled her very happy childhood, 'I still remember making a wish for brothers at the Jogi Pir mela. I had never seen such a big mela. Bhapaji sold a lot of things and he bought me a violet salwar-kameez that I was gazing greedily at. You know, violet is my favourite colour.' Suddenly the smile vanished and she told me sadly, 'I was wearing a violet-coloured suit even on that unhappy day. I returned home with the suit tattered and my dreams shattered.' It took some time for Baljit to regain her composure and talk of the times when her dreams were still unharmed.

Baljit spent most of her time with her father as her mother was coping with poor health and successive childbirths. A little sister arrived after Pammo and then their brothers. Baljit, being the eldest, was quick to help her mother in everything but, when she was eight, Bant decided that it was time that she went to school.

'I am admitting Baljit to the village school tomorrow,' Bant told his wife.

The Colour Violet

Harbans looked up, worried, 'Don't do that. How will I manage everything? Baljit helps with the four younger ones. I am still nursing Nirbhay and there is one child on the way.'

'She will go only for a few hours, then she will help you after school. Harbans, you and I never learnt to read or write but our children should. I want all my children to go to school. I don't want them to suffer the humiliation of working in others' fields.'

At home, Bant's word is law and the very next day Baljit was admitted to the village primary school where her father had heard Udasi and his songs for the first time many years earlier. Baljit's younger brothers and sisters followed in her footsteps. So while other Dalit children went to work as daily wagers in fields, Bant's children—in clean uniforms and with satchels hanging on their shoulders—attended school. The Jat landowners in the village would murmur: 'He is trying to rise above his station. He is not like the other Mazhabis. See how he dresses in trousers and shirts and sends all his children to school.'

'This will not last long. A crow can never become a swan. Soon, his dreams will turn to dust,' another would add.

'What does he have that he holds his head so high? Not even an inch of land to call his own,' yet another would say.

The Ballad of Bant Singh

Supporting a large family on just his earnings was not an easy task but Bant kept diversifying into different trades so that he could clothe, feed and educate his children. His earnings were not too much, and there were no savings, but they lived well. Bant was very enterprising and always willing to try out new schemes. One day, when he was visiting the school in Aklia, an employee read out a news item from a Punjabi paper on the economic advantage of rearing pigs. This is what led Bant to approach the Animal Husbandry Department, which was aiding pig-farming, and set up his own piggery with Yorkshire pigs. The returns were very good and Bant enjoyed looking after the pigs and would take them out grazing. 'Once I met a nomad from Bikaner who had come here to graze his sheep. Although he was a Musalman, and pigs are considered unholy and profane by the Muslims, he would be happy to see my pink pigs with their round snouts,' he recalled.

However, the Jat landlords were not happy with Bant and his pigs. They complained that the pigs swam in the same pools as their buffaloes did. The piggery closed when Bant stayed in the hospital for a year. 'The pigs were sold then. The Jats were not unhappy with the pigs but with the money that I earned through them. Each litter would fetch me twenty to twenty-five thousand per year which was the same an agrarian labourer would get. That was the real bone of contention.'

The Colour Violet

Bant possessed an indefatigable spirit and a sharp mind. 'When my father grew old and retired from his job as peon in Aklia, I would joke with him that had I gone to school, who knows what I would have become! Well, actually, he did admit me to school but I was so busy playing and being a goatherd along with my cousins that I did not bother to go to school and the family also did not worry about it.' He added, 'There was so much poverty and no awareness. Grazing goats seemed a more useful task than learning to read or write. One realizes the lost opportunity of education only when one grows up. I wanted to give this opportunity to my children.'

It was a day of joy for Bant when Baljit learnt to read and write the Gurmukhi alphabet. She moved from one class to the next and although she passed muster in studies, she showed a special talent for sports. She was always first in races and a part of the school kho-kho and kabaddi teams. Baljit had also inherited her father's talent for singing. A popular singer at school functions, she would be much in demand at weddings in the vehra. Come adolescence and Baljit started gaining height. She was soon as tall as her mother and friends started calling her 'lamboo'. The tall and slender Baljit was now a recipient of the male gaze.

Her best friend was a girl from the vehra and her namesake. To save everyone from the confusion of dealing with two Baljits, the other one was called Ballo.

The Ballad of Bant Singh

The twosome were inseparable. 'We were the best of friends in school. Once a nail went into the sole of my foot and it hurt badly, but Ballo wept more than I did. In fact, she ran ahead to give the news at home but was sobbing so loudly that she could barely convey what had happened,' recalled Baljit.

There was also a young man in Baljit's life—none other than film star Ajay Devgan. There were several television sets in the vehra but Bant did not allow his children to watch TV. 'We did manage to see some films and other programmes when Bhapaji would be away. Ballo and I always watched films together. We must have been very young when we saw him in a film called *Phool aur Kaante*.' She laughed, and confessed, 'That one film and we both lost our hearts to him.' When Baljit turned sixteen, the family decided that it was time to start looking for a boy so that she could be married off once she completed Class X and turned eighteen. Bant would have liked her to continue her studies and get a job like Udasi's daughters, but he was a practical man and realized that this might not work. She was not academically inclined but had all the qualities of a good home-maker. She had taken over many of the responsibilities of the household from her mother and was a very caring sister to her younger siblings. The climate in villages was not safe for a Dalit girl, especially so if she happened to be attractive.

The Colour Violet

It took a whole year, but a suitable boy was finally found for Baljit. He was the only son of a Dalit family slightly better off than Bant's and Baljit's life would be secure there. The day the boy and his parents were to come to see Baljit, she wore her new violet-coloured suit, printed all over with tiny white daisies. The boy and his family instantly liked her, for she was not just comely but efficient as she served them food. Baljit stole a glance at the young man, who was just three or four years older than her, and she felt that he bore a resemblance to her hero Ajay Devgan. Harbans told them how Bant had distributed sweets when she was born and everyone laughed. The date for the engagement ceremony was fixed and the news of her betrothal spread through the vehra. The marriage was to be after a year when Baljit completed her Class X, although her mother-in-law-to-be said, 'We will be happy even if you marry her at once for we are not going to send her out to work. Let her come and look after our house and be a daughter to me.'

'You are right in saying so,' said Bant, 'but it will take us some time to get ready for the marriage. Also she will complete her Class X. Anyway, now she is your daughter and we are just looking after her here.'

However, one July afternoon that year, 2002, was to change the course of Baljit's life. There was a Dalit woman in the neighbourhood called Gurmail Kaur, who

The Ballad of Bant Singh

had rented out a room to Tarsem, a medical practitioner from another village. That unhappy day, when Bant and his wife were away, Gurmail came over to Baljit requesting her to help her with some household chore. When she reached Gurmail's home she realized that a trap had been set for her. She was gagged, dragged into the house and cruelly tossed between Tarsem and Mandhir, a Jat boy from the village. Gurmail, an accomplice of the rapists, stood guard while the two raped Baljit.

Bant and Harbans found a hysterical Baljit when they got home that night, wailing and repeating, 'Bhapaji, we must kill them. We have to kill them. See what they have done to your sherni.' It was not until the next day that she could be cajoled into discarding her torn suit and bathing herself. Bant recounted, 'I did not wait for the morning and went at once to the sarpanch to report the matter and seek punishment for the guilty. It was a very difficult matter. Baljit was engaged to be married. If the news spread the engagement would be broken and what would Baljit's fate be after that? A million doubts were plaguing me but I was assured by the sarpanch that the guilty would be punished. They told me not to take the matter to the police station. The village panchayat would deliver justice.'

The general advice was to keep it quiet. 'When I told the panchayat members of my decision to take recourse to law, they advised me not to do so. "Things like this happen in the village," they said, "let the culprits compensate you monetarily and you marry off your daughter."' The rape of a minor Dalit girl is not unusual in a Punjab village. There is systematic sexual exploitation and women often have to pay the price for fetching fodder or defecating in the fields belonging to Jats as they have no fields of their own. Most cases go unreported and, sometimes, if the victim's family protests, a small monetary settlement is made and the minor girl becomes a prey for the upper castes for all time.

Meanwhile, Baljit's life had changed forever. Besides the erosion of self-esteem and extreme anger, she was quietly made to leave school and sent to some relatives in Mansa. 'Whenever I went to meet her, she said that we had to kill them. She was desolate. She had lost her honour, her home, her school and her friends. I discussed her plight with some of my Party colleagues and they too advised me to take recourse to law,' Bant recalled. Kanwaljit, a young electronics engineer who later became a full-time activist for the Liberation Party and works with agrarian labourers, said, 'It is so horrendous that in most cases the compensation does not exceed fifteen hundred to two thousand rupees.' Not just that, in many cases sexual exploitation by the landlords is an accepted fact and very often the girls do not even complain, taking it to be their fate. Minor Dalit girls become victims of rape soon after puberty. Bhagwant Rasoolpuri, a Dalit fiction writer in Punjabi, describes poignantly how a lower-caste girl is initiated into sex in his classic story, *Kasoorwar* (The Guilty):

> My childhood was ordinary, simple, like it is for most girls. When I was small, my mother thrashed me. I would refuse to go to school but she would drag me there. I barely managed to scrape through every year. I was in class six or seven when my father was paralysed. There was no source of income and my mother sent me to work with the other women from our mohalla. I was young so I only got a meagre wage. Then my mother began sending me to wash clothes and clean in the home of the England-returned family. The people of the house were kind. They gave me food and old clothes. I was helpless before their college-going son—I still tremble when I think of the first time. He used to give me food and money on the quiet. Later, I started liking it. It was then I got married to Lachhu. Perhaps the old hunchbacked grandmother of the house said something to my mother because I was asked to stop working there. It was the same quagmire of poverty in my husband's home.

Kanwaljit stresses his point: 'In a climate such as this, it becomes ridiculous to talk of the girl's consent.' Baljit's case was different because Bant had empowered his children as well as he could; he never allowed them to work in fields which belonged to the Jats, and had given them an education and a sense of self-worth. 'If I had gone on my own it would have been a different matter, but I had been tricked into it. I could have concealed it but I did not,' Baljit said.

Finally, Bant went to the police station to register a case and the local police official at Joga told him: 'Do not make this mistake, Bant. Your daughter's reputation will be ruined forever. No one will marry her. She will just become a prey to anyone and everyone's lust.' Bant's relatives were also wary and told him not get into a direct confrontation with the powerful Jats. 'We are the downtrodden and should know our station. It is not for us to fight the Jats. We cannot equal them,' was the counsel given to him.

Bant protested, 'Who says we are unequal? Guru Gobind Singh did not say so, the Constitution of our country does not say so. Then why should we keep suffering in silence? What if this was to be done to their daughters?'

So, defying the panchayat, relatives and neighbours, Bant and his daughter Baljit decided to come out in the open and seek justice. The first fallout of this decision was that Baljit's engagement had to be called off. 'We took the first step. I did not want to hide anything and cheat anyone. We called them and four members of their family came. We told them that our daughter had been raped and we were now going to court to seek justice. We said that if all this was unacceptable to them then we were willing to break the engagement,' said Bant.

Unsurprisingly, the engagement was called off. Baljit, who is honest to the point of being blunt, said, 'I still think of what happened and what could have been. I had reached a point when I had stopped feeling sorrow for the turns and twists that my life was taking. I wanted to fight and get justice for the wrong done to me. But I often think of the broken engagement, even though I have come a long way. One day that boy's mother called me and said that I could not become their daughter-in-law, but I would always be her daughter.'

The next thing that Baljit had to face was a smear campaign. Whenever any woman comes out in the open to raise the issue of sexual harassment or domestic violence, or even compete for space that is a male preserve, the first thing she has to face is being labelled 'loose' or 'promiscuous' as a part of the unsaid but very strong resistance by male-dominated society. 'Decent' girls are supposed to keep quiet and not make a public display of their humiliation. In the case of a Dalit girl, this labelling is much worse. The rape of a Dalit girl by a Jat is not considered an offense and, more often than not, it is the girl who is held to be guilty for throwing herself at the boy. The parents of the victim are advised to keep a check on their girl. The entire environment in the village or town supports such an attitude.

The media and law-enforcement agencies are no different. Dalit writer Des Raj Kali once told me that the sexual exploitation of a Dalit girl is even made out to be a favour done to her. He quoted a folk-inspired song penned by a popular Punjabi poet, Shiv Kumar Batalvi: 'Mainu Heere-Heere aakhe, hai ni munda lambdhan da' (The son of the village headman calls me Heer, darling). Heer, of course, is the eternal beloved of the love legend of Heer-Ranjha and lambdhan is derived from nambardar or lambardar, a village headman who is registered by a number in the Collectors' roll and is authorized to receive the taxes due to the government and hand them over. He is the most important man in the village and is most often from the wealthiest family of landlords. In this song, the village belle is basking in the glory of being wooed by the lambardar's son. 'My hurt with a poet as talented as Batalvi is that he is once again glorifying the males of the upper caste and class, who are often the most exploitative of women and more so of those from the lower caste,' said Kali. Many are the songs glorifying this exploitation, both old and new. In one yesteryear song, a seductive appeal is made to the lambardar: 'O pind dea lambardara, paana hi main laal ghaghra'. (Listen, headman, I wish to wear a red skirt).

The Ballad of Bant Singh

The songs dear to Baljit's heart, however, were revolutionary in nature, in which a woman wants to change her life of oppression and fight for justice. She was after all schooled in the poignant working-class songs of Sant Ram Udasi and the strong, spirited verses of Jagrup Singh Jhunir. When one hears Bant or Baljit sing Jhunir's song: 'Mere daaj vich dayin pistaul, Babula' (Give me a pistol in my dowry, my Father), the song comes alive. Legal justice became Baljit's weapon and, in the same stoic yet stubborn manner of her father, she faced every hurdle that came her way. The policemen were crude and so was the defence lawyer in court. 'However, I did not let anything deter me and whatever question their lawyer put to me, I answered without fear or shame. Main itt da jawab patthar naal ditta. (I tossed back a stone for every brick hurled at me). What need was there for me to feel ashamed? They had done a shameful act, not me,' she said with clarity and an unquenchable spirit.

~

'The tragedy of Dalit existence is that exploitation of women and girls is accepted as a part of fate and the reasons for this are economic,' Rahi said. He is educating his two daughters because he can afford to do so, but not many of his caste can. Since he has the means and the contacts, Rahi has personally involved himself in cases of atrocities against Dalits but, each time, there has been an out-of-court settlement with the victims withdrawing the case after taking a little money. 'Each time I have come out looking a fool,' he confessed. 'What makes Bant different is that he offered resistance and pursued the case. Otherwise, no one is even offering resistance in these trying times of agrarian crises when Dalit labourers are hit harder than the farmers.'

What went against Bant was that he raised his voice on vital issues when the others of his community did not speak out due to fear. It was Baljit who told me how Bant had objected to the Jat boys of the village putting up a badminton net just behind the spot where Dalit women used to squat every morning. 'The boys would come out early to play and often come very close to us searching for the shuttlecock. This was most humiliating for we were exposed to them. Others just kept quiet but my Bhapaji went to them and asked them to move the net elsewhere, but they refused to do so. Some time later the net was pulled out and thrown away. The boys came to my father accusing him of having done so. He told them that he would never fight like a jackal,' said Baljit. In fact, it would be in order if he had pulled out the net because the upper-caste boys did not have the grace to respect the privacy of women, but that was not the case. Later, the person responsible for pulling out and throwing away the net was identified, yet the boys held on to their grouse against Bant because he was the one bold enough to openly check them.

I have a dear Jat friend who also belongs to Bant's village. Even he exhibited the same casual, feudal attitude to the sexual exploitation of Dalit girls. Brushing aside any question of rape, he declared that the girl had given her consent. What is surprising is that my friend chose to ignore the fact that sex with a girl below eighteen is counted as rape as per the law of the land and thus there is no question of consent by a minor. And, when asked to comment about the expolitation of Dalit girls in general, he said, 'Well, you see, Dalit girls like Jat boys!' In a sense, it was almost as if one should sympathize with the helpless Jat boys who have to oblige Dalit girls by raping them.

According to Rahi, the so-called 'liking' is deeply rooted in the socio-economic climate. 'It is basically a liasion of the haves and have-nots. As soon as Dalit girls reach puberty, Jat boys start "wooing" them in the fields and they become easy prey because of their poverty and low self-esteem.' However, what perturbs him most is that the resistance to exploitation of this kind, which had been built up by social and Left movements, is totally lost in the present time.

There was now a hurry to marry Baljit off. She had already been moved out of the village to live with relatives in Bathinda. They found a match for her there—

The Colour Violet

Resham, an agrarian labourer from Sirsa, who was a widower with a ten-year-old son and who was much older than Baljit. However, he was willing to accept her as his wife even though he was told what had befallen her. Thus, while the case was in progress at the Mansa Sessions Court, Baljit's marriage was arranged to Resham. It was a quiet wedding for Baljit, with the groom just putting a veil on her and taking her as his bride. There was no feasting and no singing. The court pronounced the sentence of life imprisonment upon the three accused, including Gurmail Kaur and, with the satisfaction of having received justice, Baljit went on with her life as a home-maker.

'Resham has been good to me and we are well adjusted. He does not take any intoxicants and gives all his earnings to me. What more can one ask for?' she said in the tone of a woman who has learned to come to terms with the harsh realities of life. Although her husband stood by her, other members of the family were not as supportive. Her mother-in-law would never lose an opportunity to throw the gang-rape in her face and also curse her son for marrying a 'fallen' woman. 'She still will not stop doing so, and although I have learned to ignore her, sometimes it does hurt. I will not lie to you but I often find myself unhappy at the injustice that was done to me and I refuse to call it fate. Then I tell Resham that I want to kill those three people,' she confessed. Baljit is a mother of three and also fond of her stepson who lives with his maternal grandparents. 'When my mother-in-law failed to poison my husband's mind, she tried to turn my stepson against me. When he comes visiting, if I have cooked something nice and want to share it with him, she will ask him not to take it for I may be trying to poison him. So one day I mixed the food in one thali and asked all the four children to eat together so that if I had put poison in the food then they too would die.'

Baljit is a fighter and Bant could not have prepared his daughter better to face the struggles of life. She is quite open in voicing the truth about her parents too. 'They did not give me anything at the time of my marriage: no clothes, no utensils, no bedding. Their means were limited but even so no effort was made to do all this because Resham was a widower and they were relieved that I should be married and secure after what had happened to me. But if you come to Sirsa, visit my village home and you will find that I have everything. Resham and I have worked hard to provide for our children.' She added that for people in the village, she is an example to be held up, for she was a girl who had built a home out of nothing. She has also taken the initiative to plan her family by getting herself operated upon after the birth of her third child.

Not just that, she has always been there for her

The Colour Violet

parental family. After the assault on Bant, she left her own home to be with her younger sisters and brothers. 'I am very attached to all of them.' She told me this as we sat on the rooftop of Bant's house and chatted. She pointed to Gurmail Kaur's house just across from Bant's. 'They did not consult me before buying land to build a new house otherwise I would not have let them. One should have better neighbours.' Over the years, Baljit has become very engrossed in her own home, taking care of her husband, two sons and a daughter. Now a buffalo has been added to the household. Bant, realizing that his eldest daughter was married without gifts from her parents, sent one buffalo to Resham and Baljit so that his grandchildren get plenty of milk.

I asked if she felt happy that her father had distributed sweets at her birth. 'Yes,' she replied with a smile, 'I was in my parents' home when my daughter Amanpreet was born because Bhapaji was in the hospital. Otherwise, I would have distributed sweets at her birth too.'

In every way her father's daughter, Baljit has shown great courage in re-building her broken life. Often, when words fail me, some poem stored away in my mind comes to my aid. In expressing the wonder I feel for this girl, I find myself recalling a poem in which my favourite poet Kumar Vikal has captured the soul of a Santhal girl:

The Ballad of Bant Singh

Ji, meri kavita gaurvarna nahin
Zara sanwali si hai
Ek Santhal bachchi ki tarhan khurdari
Jo badhi ho kar
Gulabi frock nahi pehanegi
Ice-cream nahi khayegi
Titli nahi kehalayegi
Nange paanv hi apne logon ke beech bhaag jaayegi…

Yes, my poem is not fair-skinned
She is somewhat dark
Rough like a Santhal baby girl
She will not grow up to wear a pink frock or eat ice-cream
She will never be called a butterfly
Barefoot, she will run to her own people…

Baljit is now among her own people, she is a wife, a mother, a step-mother, a dutiful daughter, a fond older sister, a home maker, an activist—all this only at twenty-five. Yes, her body remembers—bodies of Dalit girls too have a memory—as does her mind, the battering they received at a time when all she could think of was winning at athletics and imagine that her fiance resembled Ajay Devgan. She has come through in her own way and still has the heart and the courage to say: 'My favourite colour is violet'.

~

The Colour Violet

Baljit remains an exception to the rule. There are thousands of others wallowing in the humiliation that they have had to undergo. In August 2010, there was a report in all major newspapers of a Dalit woman being paraded naked in Bhagwanpur village near Batala. An influential family from the neighbourhood took her to their house, beat her up and tore off her clothes. She was then forced to march around the village naked. All this because the family suspected her brother-in-law of having an affair with a girl from their family. The police reluctantly registered a case once they failed to convince the woman to reach a compromise with the accused family. There was yet another report of a minor Dalit girl being kidnapped and raped in Batala town in Gurdaspur district. The victim, a student of Class X who was on her way to buy some groceries, was forcibly picked up by some motorcycle-borne youths.

As opposed to the songs glorifying the lambardar and his sons, there is a very moving song by Sant Ram Udasi of the first marital night of a labourer girl who speaks of the bangles on her virgin wrists having already been shattered and prays: 'Phir na koi putt lambrhan da roop kirat da choosay' (May no son of the lambardars suck up the beauty of a labourer girl). This poem was narrated to me by Rajinder Rahi. After reading out another poem by Udasi, in which a Dalit girl talks of her sister-in-law's molestation in the landlord's haveli where she goes to do menial work, Rajinder Rahi said: 'In modern times, the haveli has been replaced by the SUV, in which Dalit girls and women are not only picked up and raped, they are also kidnapped and trafficked.' Rahi gives one more instance of how tradition has sanctioned the abuse of Dalit girls in different ways. 'In our parts the tradition was that at the time of Dalit marriages one night of dance by women of the maternal family was reserved for the pleasure of the Jat boys. They would come and sing out often risqué bolis to which the women had to dance the giddha. They would put songs of their choice on loudspeakers.' Rahi's father Sardar Kartar Singh Nirdharak, an activist of the Laal Party who was vigorously involved in the Mujahara movement aimed at allotting land to the landless tillers of the soil, brought an end to this practice.

Tradition and myth sanctify the sexual exploitation of Dalit girls in different ways. Discussing this with my colleagues in our office in Mohali near Chandigarh, I learnt of another such myth. Amarjit Singh, a young computer operator who also happens to be a Jat, told me that in his village of Bherwal in Patiala district, the prevalent myth is that if a Jat male has sex with a virgin Dalit girl, he will be immune to ailments of the eye, nose and throat, even headaches. He added in all innocence, 'My chacha has such relations with Dalit girls and we have never seen him fall sick.' Rahi said, 'Under the sway of the progressive and Left movements there was an effort to raise the dignity of the Dalits. During my father's time, no upper-caste male could dare to come to the vehra to seek favours from a Dalit woman. They may have met stealthily in the fields but never openly in the residential areas. But now it is a free for all and Dalit women have been reduced to the role of poorly-paid prostitutes, even in villages.'

Later, as Bant and I shared a cab that I hired from Chandigarh to see the samadhi of Jogi Pir, Bant put matters more bluntly, in his trademark style, 'The girls who dance at weddings and parties where currency notes are showered on them are neither daughters of Badal nor the Kaptan (Capt. Amarinder Singh). They are the daughters of Dalit labourers, but I dare not say this.'

The driver of the cab, Hukam Singh, a Ravidasia, was quick to respond: 'Best not to say it. Never mind Badal or Kaptan, our own people will blame you for snatching away their morsels of food.'

This is the sad reality of Dalit girls in many areas of Punjab. Vishav Bharti, a young Chandigarh-based journalist who received a fellowship for a rural journalism project to study the impact of the agricultural crises on the lives of agrarian labourers, writes: 'The crisis of the labour community isn't just one generation's suffering. Pushed out of agriculture, the quest for survival has turned the "GenNext" of Dalit agricultural labourers into waiters, prostitutes and dancers.'

The Ballad of Bant Singh

The case from which Bharti drew his conclusion related to one Gurpreet Kaur, the daughter of a daily wager from Lambi village near Bathinda. Divorced from her labourer husband, she took on work as an orchestra dancer. Her parents were so ashamed that she was not allowed to come home for two years, but now she is their bread-winner even though precautions are taken so that she does not perform near her own village. Gurpreet is not the only one. The past decade has seen scores of very poor Dalit girls from the villages of the Cotton Belt reaching Bathinda to become singers, dancers and even prostitutes.

There are very few occasions in the lives of rural workers when they can celebrate with their relatives and community. Weddings are the most prominent of them and marrying off a daughter from home is a matter of pride for a rural labourer in Punjab. But with conditions having worsened for everyone connected with the business of agriculture, the weddings of daughters have become a burden. It is easy to find girls long past marriageable age, simply because their parents couldn't afford to marry them off. So small-town clubs, religious institutions, NRIs, NGOs, business associations and politicians have taken up the task of organizing mass weddings and garnering media attention. Rahi laments, 'Even the honour of sending a girl away from her home is gone. There have been cases when in the crowd of mass marriages brides nearly went away with the wrong grooms. Other times the ceremonies have to be postponed abruptly at the last minute as the chief guest, invariably a politician, has been held up at the last minute.'

In Udasi's song, the girl entreats her mother to not give birth to her in a village where her dreams will forever be shackled. If there is any village in my Punjab where this does not happen, I would like to know its name.

The Making of a Movement

Embracing the labourer, the farmer wept,
Water flowed even from hay

—Udasi

WHEN SANT RAM UDASI wrote this song in the seventies, it stirred the hearts of all Punjabis as it referred to the collective sorrows of an agrarian community. The allusion was to the times before the advent of mechanized farming when the farmer and labourer worked together to till the soil. If some calamity struck and the crop was lost, the two shared the sorrow, for the sweat of both would have soaked into the earth. However, Udasi reinterpreted this togetherness in the context of the farmers and labourers coming together in the fold of Leftist movement aimed at creating a more equal social order which would address shared sorrows. It was this song that came to Sukhdarshan Natt's mind as he stood with his hand on Bant's shoulder as the latter lay bandaged in the Mansa Civil Hospital. The two had known each other since their youth and, together, they had pledged to work for a society which would not work for the advantage of one section and the disadvantage of another. Both were strong men in different ways so there was no question of a display of any sorrow but, deep inside, they felt a shared grief. The battering of Bant's body was also the shattering of the shared dreams of co-travellers.

The Ballad of Bant Singh

As the day progressed, the sorrow which Natt and other comrades of Bant felt turned into anger. They realized that a heinous crime had been committed, but there was no one on their side, neither the police nor the press. The doctors seemed indifferent to Bant's plight. It was a battle that was close to being lost.

The landlord-police nexus had done its job efficiently. The local police registered a case under Section 325 of the Indian Penal Code (voluntarily causing grievous hurt) and released the accused on bail. This was done in complete disregard of the medico-legal report which listed some twenty injuries on Bant's limbs. As the day progressed, the doctors showed little concern or anxiety about Bant's condition. Party colleague Jasbir Natt recalled: 'All they kept doing was changing bandages from time to time.' Bant's comrades made the rounds of the local reporters in Mansa but no one seemed interested in taking any notice. Gurjant Singh recounted the frustration: 'The brutal attack on Bant had been blacked out. By the third day in the hospital, the closing ranks of the system were clearly visible. We lost all hope from the local police, the doctors and also the press.'

Then, after thirty-six long hours, the authorities at the hospital said that they were unable to treat Bant and that he should be moved to either Patiala or Chandigarh. In the words of Beant Akali, 'There was an urgent meeting in the hospital corridors and the late Jeeta

Kaur, who was then the state coordinator of the Party, said that Bant was to be moved to Patiala or Chandigarh at once. His comrades contributed five thousand rupees each and so did I even though I am an Akali. My only concern was that the poor man's life should be saved.'

It was a caravan of sorts that started for Patiala, as it was closer than Chandigarh. Bant was accompanied by his wife and older brother, Party colleagues and saviour Beant. Some contacts had been alerted in Rajendra Hospital and a team of doctors was already waiting to examine him outside the Emergency ward. They had a quick look at his injuries, the gangerene that had set in, and advised that he be rushed to the Postgraduate Institute of Medical Sciences and Research (PGIMER) in Chandigarh as his condition was far too serious.

Young Kanwaljit, the electronics engineer who had learnt robot-making at the Central Scientific Instruments Organisation in Chandigarh, recounted: 'I forgot all about robot-making when I came face to face with Bant who was lying on the stretcher in a corridor of the PGI late night on 7 January in a terrible state. Yet he looked up at me and smiled.'

'As long as a Comrade's throat is not slit it is all right. The rest can be taken care of,' Bant told this young activist.

Kanwaljit was an engineer by day and an activist by night. Coming from a family affiliated to the Communist

The Ballad of Bant Singh

Party of India (Marxist) (CPI-M), he had chosen to work with the Liberation ML group as it was doing significant work in Punjab. He had been alerted to be present when Bant and others reached the PGI.

'His arms and legs were black and swollen and it did not seem that he would survive. But when he smiled and talked hopefully, I had a feeling that he would. Such a man could not die,' said Kanwaljit.

Medical attendance was quick and, fearing that Bant's life was in danger, the doctors had to take a prompt decision. They said that both his arms and one leg would be amputated but they would try to save one leg. However, they admitted that there was no guarantee that they would be able to do so. Kanwaljit was entrusted with the very difficult task of conveying these sad tidings to Bant. 'It had to be told so I did so. Bant shed no tears. He looked away for a few moments, as though he was thinking of someone else's predicament, and then he looked me straight in the eye. He said then, "I suppose the doctors know best. Anyway what use are my arms and legs, I have to sing with my throat."'

But Bant is only human, and he did shed tears, but only when Harbans came to his side.

'When he told me that the doctors had no choice but to amputate his limbs, tears flowed down his cheeks and I knew he was thinking of our children and I. How would he fend for us? I wiped his tears and put my hand on his chest. But as soon as I came out of the room, I got a piercing ache in my head and felt dizzy. I lay down on a bench. I did not know when I passed out. I had suffered a paralytic attack.'

Bant lost three limbs on 8 January and, as he was moved into intensive care, his comrades, after recovering from the grave shock, got busy in organizing the struggle for justice. One of the first steps was to appeal to the police authorities for sterner action against the culprits, with recommendations from the doctors at PGI that Bant's life was still in danger. The next was to hold a press conference in the basement of Punjab Book Centre in Chandigarh's Sector 22 on 11 January. The *Times of India* carried a story in which correspondent Ramaninder Kaur brought out the grave injustice in no uncertain terms: 'In a country where law-breakers excel in subverting the system, how much is a landless farm worker expected to pay for getting justice for his minor rape-victim daughter? To be precise, two arms and a leg.' Other papers followed and the blackout which the Mansa reporters had imposed gradually lifted. This brought a sad reflection from Comrade Jeeta: 'After the attack, we contacted the media but even the local papers did not report the beating up of a Dalit. It was only when his limbs were amputated that journalists seemed to find the incident newsworthy.' Tragic indeed are the yardsticks of news-making, but the reports on Bant

The Ballad of Bant Singh

soon flared into outrage and the collective conscience was roused from apathy because it was not just one man's tale—Bant emerged as a symbol of Dalit resistance in Punjab.

Meanwhile, Bant's older brother, Hansa Singh, became an important witness in the assault on Bant Singh. Before the final brutal attack on him, the boys had assaulted him twice but Bant had got away with minor injuries. It was then that Hansa had heard the influential former sarpanch, Naranjan Singh, say, 'If you had to beat him, you should have broken his arms and legs. We would have bailed you out anyway but this swine would have been taught a lesson for all time. What was the point in letting him off with a few bruises?' After the youths assaulted him so that not a bone was left unbroken, Hansa made a statement to the police. This led to Naranjan Singh being rounded up but, later, Hansa went back on his statement. Bant's Party colleagues said that he had been bought over for just a couple of thousand of rupees. Hansa was not just bought over, he was threatened until he finally turned hostile and fled the village to live in Pitho village near Rampura Phull where one of their sisters was married. It was there that he expired some years later. Nevertheless, Beant Akali recalled with glee the nabbing of the former sarpanch. 'He was let off later as there was no evidence, but the day he was put in the lock up, people gathered at my home to celebrate and we had a big display of fireworks.'

However, sorrow and silence sat heavily on Bant's home. Baljit had arrived with her three-month-old baby, Satnam, to look after her brothers and sisters as their mother was with Bant in Chandigarh. 'I did not leave my husband's side even for a day. Baljit looked after the children and for a long time we did not let the younger children know that their father now was without his arms and a leg,' Harbans said.

But when the youngest, Jagmeet—Paroche—learnt the harsh reality, he looked up at his eldest sister and asked in desolation: 'Will Bhapaji never take me in his arms now? Will he never be able to pick me up?'

Now it is Paroche who serves as willing arms to Bant, holding a cellphone to his ears, raising a glass of tea to his lips, fanning away flies on hot summer days, and scratching his back.

A letter from the Delhi-based Forum for Democratic Initiatives (FDI) Front—signed by activist Radhika Menon and eight hundred and twenty-three other signatories—to Prime Minister Manmohan Singh, with a copy to then Punjab chief minister Amarinder Singh led to some action by the police.

Dear Prime Minister,
   We the undersigned condemn the savage and barbaric assault by powerful Congress-backed Jat

The Ballad of Bant Singh

landlords which has left Bant Singh, Dalit leader of the Mazdoor Mukti Morcha (All-India Agrarian Labour Association) in Mansa, Punjab, with both hands and one leg amputated. Further we note that this criminal attack was planned in retaliation for Bant Singh's sustained campaign against caste and gender based power and violence, and in particular, his struggle to bring his minor daughter's rapists to justice. We stand by Bant Singh and his family in the face of this unspeakable tragedy and we believe passionately that such atrocities cannot be acceptable in 21st century India.

1. We urge you to accord the highest priority to the medical treatment and rehabilitation of Bant Singh, in particular the provision of artificial limbs to him at an appropriate stage. This has to be undertaken irrespective of the costs or effort involved. Further, the rehabilitation will have to consider also the living conditions, livelihood and insurance against future ailments arising from Bant Singh's current disabilities.

2. We urge you to immediately organise the payment of due compensation for Bant Singh and his family in order to alleviate the great suffering caused by the assault, again keeping in mind all future needs.

3. While police authorities have, under under great public pressure, arrested seven youths who have allegedly been involved in the assault on Bant Singh, no efforts must be spared to bring those who masterminded the attack to justice. We demand an

The Making of a Movement

independent inquiry into the incident to ascertain whether the Punjab government is shielding prominent people involved in planning the attack due to their affiliation with the ruling Congress Party.

4. We are deeply concerned by the attempts by senior police officials to dismiss any link between the attacks on Bant Singh and his courageous struggle against those who raped his minor daughter in 2002. The successful sentencing of the rapists to life imprisonment by a Sessions Court in 2004 is a very strong motive for the repeated assaults by upper-caste men on Bant Singh over the past year, and must not be swept aside as irrelevant to the case.

5. The Bant Singh incident is the tip of the iceberg as far as atrocities on Dalits in Punjab are concerned. Apart from the severe economic exploitation of Dalits, who form a very large percentage of all agricultural labour in the state, there is systematic sexual exploitation of Dalit women. This is a matter for immediate inquiry for the SC/ST Commission, the National Human Rights Commission as well as the National Women's Commission.

A movement was in the making. The intervention of senior police officers led to the upgradation of the case to 308 of the Indian Penal Code (attempt to commit culpable homicide) and the accused were arrested. As Ramaninder went to her office to file the report after the press conference, DIG P. S. Sarao informed the

The Ballad of Bant Singh

Times of India that the relevant sections under the Scheduled Caste/Scheduled Tribe Act had been added to it. He added that when the news of the amputation of his limbs reached Mansa, a policeman was despatched to take Bant's statement in Chandigarh, but he was not allowed to meet the victim on medical advice.

~

A rally of agricultural workers demanding justice and compensation for Bant was called at his village on 16 January, 2006, while he was still in intensive care at the PGI. But the terror unleashed by the brutal attack took its toll on the attendance and only some five hundred activists from different outfits trickled in. However, the tide had turned within nine days. The rally on 25 January had a phenomenal attendance with over ten thousand agricultural labourers and activists. Recalling the mammoth gathering, Kanwaljit recalls that the most emotive moment came when Baljit got up, holding her three-month-old baby in her arms and spoke out in angst. He said, 'Comrade Swapan Mukherjee, who had come from Delhi, saw Baljit and asked her to speak. Without any hesitation she got up and said what had happened to her and now what had been done to her father. "How long will we suffer such injustice," she cried out and tears sprang to many eyes. It was an act of great courage because a girl in Punjab never speaks of

The Making of a Movement

any sexual exploitation, but here was someone breaking a taboo and calling out for justice.' Bant had supporters in Punjab and elsewhere. The Forum for Democratic Initiatives sent a team to Punjab to enquire into the details of the incident and launched a nation-wide campaign which laid bare the ugly face of prosperous Punjab.

Above all, it was Bant's spirit which made the movement. On the eighteenth day after his amputation, while his condition was still serious, he surprised doctors and his fellow patients alike by singing some of Udasi's songs from his sick-bed. 'That was the moment,' said Kanwaljit, 'when I decided: no more robot-making; it was time to quit my job and become a whole-timer with the Party because here I was now in the company of crusaders, the real men and women.' He has since organized agrarian labour in the Sangrur district and has not regretted the decision even for a moment. Bant and he share a special bond, because during the three months that Bant was in PGI they were constant companions. Kanwaljit says that Bant endeared himself to everyone in the hospital with his wit, humour and courage.

Annie Zaidi in her book *Known Turf* relates poignantly the notes she made in her diary after filing a magazine report:

The Ballad of Bant Singh

How does one react to a man who is lying in the hospital minus three limbs? How are you supposed to look as you step into a government hospital's trauma ward? Do you look at the bandages, staring at the parts stained red? Or do you look away into his eyes? Are you supposed to look extra-cheery or defrentially sombre? Are you supposed to sit down beside him, talk about the accident in great detail, or do you stand awkwardly, say commiserating nothings and then leave as soon as you have the information you need because...because what can you say anyway?

And what do you do when a man minus three limbs in a government hospital's trauma ward begins to sing?

Quite simple, really—you salute his spirit. And this is precisely what happened, not just in the country but abroad too. Rallies in support of Bant took place both in India and elsewhere. British South Asian groups organized a protest outside the Indian High Commission in London demanding justice for Bant. If the district-level media had tried to black him out, the international media was now clamouring for Bant's story. *Tehelka* magazine's campaign for Bant, in which readers were asked to contribute help, received an overwhelming response. 'It was with this money that we were able to purchase a plot and build a new house for Bant where he would have space to live in and air to breathe,' said Sukhdarshan Natt.

The Making of a Movement

The reactions of the readers of the *Tehelka* story, who contributed to the Bant fund, indicated the changing mood of the times and a guilty conscience. Sheoraj Singh Bechain of New Delhi said: 'In spite of being one of the most developed states of the country, Punjab still has landlordism. Bant Singh's story testifies to the existence there of the caste system too. Every secular and progressive person of this country should support him. In fact, I felt guilty at sending in my contribution two months late.' Kunal Kapoor of Mumbai wrote: 'We hear of injustice but do nothing about it. But Bant Singh did. He had everything to lose and he lost everything, including his motion. But he still went on and on. He is one of a kind. In what he has done, he is an inspiration to many of us.' The money collected was given to Bant at a function held in Mansa later that year. Showing pictures taken at the function by Raghu Rai, Bant recounted with a laugh: 'Raghu told me that when he was asked to photograph a man who was without three limbs, he wondered what kind of pictures he would be able to click but he got such wonderful frames.'

While Left-wing groups and other democratic organizations were making efforts to get justice for Bant, a parallel effort was being made by the accused, who had the backing of the local power structures and the upper-caste psyche, to establish that the rape was one matter and the physical assault quite another. Never mind the

The Ballad of Bant Singh

fact that these were directed against the same man—to him directly, or through his daughter, to him. A major effort was underway to establish that caste prejudice had no role in the entire episode. Disinformation was rampant and there was an endeavour to establish that only four of the seven accused were actually involved in the attack and three had been implicated falsely. One of the saddest documents was a fact-finding report released by Ved Prakash Gupta, 'allegedly' a former Naxalite and then the self-styled general secretary of the Punjab Human Rights Committee. It was released on 17 April, 2006 and the contents speak for themselves. One wonders why Gupta and company were not put behind bars for contempt of court and mockery of justice. Some extracts from the report:

> The members of Punjab Human Rights Committee (PHRC), like thousands of other people were so overwhelmed by the sensational reports in many news papers including the prestigious Times Of India and Tehelka about the alleged gang rape of Bant Singh's daughter in Village Burj Jhabbar, subsequent beating of Bant Singh by upper class farmers resulting in amputation of three limbs at PGI Chandigarh, that members of PHRC did not feel the necessity of investigating the gruesome case of Bant Singh. The rat race of many political, trade unions, kisan leaders and other self promoting persons started towards the village Burj Jhabbar in support of Bant Singh a

The Making of a Movement

poor Dalit of that village to get cheap publicity that we the members of PHRC lost whatever simmering will we had to visit the village to find out what has really happened and to uncover the truth. So this much delay in sifting lies from truth is regretted and we feel guilty of this delay.

Bant Singh is a poor Dalit living in village Burj Jhabbar. He earns his living by keeping pigs and doing menial work. To begin with he was connected to Bahujan Samaj Party later shifting his loyalties to different political groups operating out side the village at different times.

Villagers told PHRC team that Mandhir Singh, son of a small poor farmer and daughter of Bant Singh were school mates before 2002. A friendship developed between the two. Both started meeting in the house of Bant Singh's sister-in-law in relation Gurmail Kaur. Another Dalit Tarsem Singh who practiced medicine was also in this company. One night Bant Singh came to know about the presence of Mandhir Singh and his daughter in the house of Gurmail Kaur. The rumour about the relationship between Bant's daughter and poor farmer's son spread like a wild fire in Burj Jhabbar, a small and backward village with only 700 votes. The elders and well meaning persons of the village tried to bring about compromise between the two families. In the mean time this rumour reached the police station. The police demanded money from Mandhir's poor father to hush up the case. The inability of the poor farmer

The Ballad of Bant Singh

to pay bribe to the police led to the registration of a rape case against Mandhir Singh, Gurmail Kaur and a Dalit Tarsem Singh on August 8, 2002. The case was registered about a month after both were caught by Bant Singh in the house of Gurmail Kaur. On July 19, 2004 all the three Mandhir Singh, Gurmail Kaur and Tarsem Singh were sent to jail for life by The Additional District and Sessions Judge, Mansa.

Villagers told the PHRC team about the alleged old rivalry between one Beant Singh (Akali) and the other Niranjan Singh (Congress). Both allegedly exploited poor Dalits in the village for their cheap political gains from time to time. One Chand Kaur a Dalit women with the support of Niranjan Singh (Congress) lodged a complaint with the police against Beant Singh and some of his supporters for injuring her. The police registered a case against Beant Singh and others under section 326, 324, 323, 148, 149 etc. The court sentenced Beant Singh and his supporters to one year imprisonment on October 11, 2004. The appeal of the case is pending in the Court at Mansa.

One day one young man Appi, who is not related to any of the above people or any group in the village, was driving scooter towards village Joga. He met with an accident involving pigs of Bant Singh on the way. Bant Singh without waiting for any explanation struck a lathi blow on the youth and insulted him. Another villager Baldev Singh a local leader of Kisan Union (Ughrahn Group) who tried to pacify Bant Singh also got hurt. The matter went to the police and both were challaned under section 107/151.

The Making of a Movement

Appi unable to digest his humiliation and insult by poor Dalit Bant Singh gathered a few of his friends and severely beat Bant Singh with the handle of a water pump on January 5th, 2006. On January 7, 2006 a case was registered at Joga police station against eight persons including former sarpanch Niranjan Singh under section 307, 308, 325, 323, 148, 149, 120B and section Â¾ of Dalits Atrocities Act. Villagers told PHRC team that Beant Singh taking advantage of attack on Bant Singh succeeded in settling old scores by inciting Bant Singh to frame Niranjan Singh and three others in the attack. Niranjan Singh got bail from High Court and all others are in Bathinda central jail. Villagers told PHRC team that Niranjan Singh, Sandeep, Balbir and Didar Singh have been named wrongly in the case and were not involved in the attack. The villagers passed a resolution on April 2, 2006 demanding the release of these four. A Dalit panchayat member and Bant's neighbors Ghamdoor Singh told the PHRC in the presence of large number of villagers the rape case and attack on Bant Singh was not at all related to each other. None of the attackers was related to persons convicted in rape case...

...The stories published by English weekly *Tehelka* from Delhi broke all records of sensationalizing the false reports. Much more oil was poured in already media created fire of caste divide and atrocities on Dalits. Tehelka created and completed picture of divide between the Dalits and

The Ballad of Bant Singh

upper caste jats in the village Burj Jhabbar and turned a small village into a battle ground of revolutionary struggle against all atrocities upon poor Dalits where none existed. Tehelka went to the extent even of opening a fund column for Bant Singh's aid. PHRC feels that perhaps it is for the first time in recent memory that press and media behaved with such carelessness and irresponsibility.

However, the Action Committee formed to seek justice did not let this, or any other such attempt, dampen its spirits. A rally was called in Chandigarh on 25 March 2006. It was a mammoth gathering where celebrated Left-wing theatre veteran, the late Gursharan Singh, had put together an emotive play on Bant's struggle called *Hik te Deeva Baal ke Rakhna* (Keeping the Lamp Aflame in the Heart). But the real surprise came when Bant himself turned up to tell his story and to sing. Bant recalled later, 'The people were moved to tears by Gursharan Singh's play and I sang as many as three songs. First the doctors were hesitant to send me to the rally but I told them that singing would heal me faster and they believed me.'

By then the movement to secure justice for Bant had gathered momentum and a senior advocate and general secretary of the Panchkula—the satellite town of Chandigarh in Haryana—chapter of the People's Union for Civil Liberties (PUCL), filed a Public Interest

The Making of a Movement

Litigation (PIL) in the Punjab and Haryana Court in Chandigarh, demanding an immediate compensation of ten lakh rupees from the Punjab government for Bant. Natt said: 'This came as a surprise to us because we did not know the advocate at all. He filed the writ on his own and this helped Bant get early financial help with the then chief minister, Captain Amarinder Singh, releasing eight lakhs from his discretionary fund.' Reading the advocate's address in the writ, I realized that he lived in my neighbourhood in Panchkula. When I went to his residence to meet him, his wife told me that he had suffered dementia two years earlier but he still remembered many of the public interest litigations which he had filed. When he filed the writ for Bant he clearly pointed out, 'It was a fit case for proceedings under contempt of court too, as the assault followed the trial court verdict.'

Meanwhile, Punjab Police made amends for the callousness initially shown by lower-ranked policemen at the Joga Police Station. The inspector general of police (IGP) of the Ferozepur range, Joginder Singh, and the senior superintendent of police, Mansa, Amit Prasad, visited Bant Singh's home and finding his dependents in dire straits made efforts to help them. Beant Akali recalled, 'Amit Prasad shamed the Joga policemen for conniving with the culprits in so heinous a crime against a man who was the only bread-winner of his family.' A detailed relief programme was chalked out and instant help given by way of bedding and rations. The two milk-yielding buffaloes which the police provided to the family were the best way of ensuring a daily income. Bant's third son Manjit was enrolled in the Police Public School in Bathinda. Prasad who visited Bant in the PGI told mediapersons, 'The idea behind our effort is to give a befitting reply to any group which metes out such extreme injustice to any other person. It could be anyone; we would do the same whether it was a case of the Dalits assaulting a Jat.' The buffaloes have multiplied since and occupy centrestage in Bant's courtyard. It is also a matter of great joy to Bant that he has given one buffalo to Baljit and now his grandchildren will never be in want of milk. However Manjit, who was doing well in both studies and sports at the police school in Bathinda, had to return home because his school had shut its hostel down. Harbans said, 'The school authorities said that he could continue but as a day scholar. We could not take this risk because he is young—and what if someone assaulted him.' Manjit, who now attends school in Joga and plays kabaddi in the evenings, said, with the determination characteristic of his family: 'I will never give up my studies.'

~

The Making of a Movement

After three months in the PGI and ten months at the Mansa Civil Hospital—receiving proper medical attention this time, after Bant's comrades staged many protests against the doctor who had taken a bribe to admit him, and had then given him little or no treatment, and had the doctor suspended—Bant was moved to the St. Stephen's Hospital in Delhi with the support of the Forum for Democratic Initiatives. The move was necessary because the amputated leg was not healing and a major surgery was required to join two broken bones. Radhika Menon also started a campaign to collect funds for his treatment and to fit him with artificial limbs. 'There is basically a lack of concern on the part of the government for the welfare of ordinary working people who lose their limbs to violence or in accidents and this needs to be urgently redressed,' she said. Bant was fitted with an artificial leg but in the absence of arms, he found it difficult to maintain balance. The next plan was to fit Bant with one electro-mechanical arm from the reputed manufacturer of prosthetic limbs from Germany, Otto Bock, while the other prosthetic was to be a less sophisticated device meant to provide only basic support. A decision was taken to provide him with other devices which could improve his quality of life and make him as independent as possible, at a future date, depending on the availability of funds.

A cultural evening was organized in Delhi to gather

funds for these limbs that were to be imported. The effort received overwhelming response and, lauding Bant's spirit of resistance, writer Arundhati Roy described the efforts to rehabilitate Bant Singh as a political act. She said, 'Bant Singh must be given back political limbs because they were smashed and taken away as part of a political act. There would be those who would want to depoliticise his rehabilitation but that his rehabilitation would be incomplete without knowing the context of his struggles.' The context of his struggles came through beautifully in the form of *A Video Letter from Bant Singh*, a seven-minute film by well-known documentary film-maker Sanjay Kak, which is counted among his best works. Looking back, Kak said: 'I had not gone there to make a film. Since Bant was not in a state to attend the function, Radhika and a few other friends asked me to make a video recording of his that could be shown there. Since the hospital did not allow any filming, a few friends kept the nurses and other hospital staff at bay and I set the camera and started shooting. The entire exercise was done in some twenty minutes. Why the film touched everyone and continues to move people is because of the genuineness of what Bant said and sang. Not much editing was done and a rough cut was shown but it worked. I would say Bant and not I made the film.'

Indeed, Bant comes through just as he is—charged,

strangely illuminated and fearless—and there he ceases to be just an individual but transforms into a symbol of a collective struggle against oppression. The film has him telling his story in few words without fuss and calling out spontaneously to every oppressed person: 'Let us all become Bhagat Singh.' A few words and he breaks into song, songs very close to his heart because they speak of the misery of the oppressed and call for change. When he sings the song of Jagrup Singh Jhunir, about a daughter who asks her father to give her a pistol in her dowry, the listener is shaken out of centuries of complacency:

> Should I not tell the truth, my father?
> How long will I bear these lies
> and suppress even my breath?
> We must reach our destination
> Don't wander away, my father
> Give me a pistol in my dowry
>
> In our villages traditions spread
> like cobwebs
> My simple mother
> Let daughters not be born in villages
> Where desires are sold with dowries
> My father, give me a pistol in my dowry!

On 4 February 2007, on a break from the Delhi hospital and campaigning for a party colleague at Budhalada near Mansa, Bant received robust rounds of applause when he lifted the Party flag with the Otto Bock hand from Germany. However, the artificial limbs never became a part of him, for he chose not to return to the hospital, get used to the artificial limbs, or get them altered to suit him better. 'I was tired of lying in hospital beds,' he said. 'I wanted to be among my people, campaigning, organizing workers and singing. I sing with my throat and my Comrades are my arms and legs.'

Song Sung Red

We will uproot oppression at the cost of our roots, my people!
Let's remould our lives in the furnace of struggle

—Udasi

THE SUN WAS gently straining through the wide but sparse foliage of the old keekar tree in the courtyard of Bant Singh's home. A new dwelling, built with help that poured in from different quarters, had replaced the old tenement in the interior of the vehra. The two goats being fattened for Bant's third daughter Sukhminder's wedding in the coming winter stood tied to a post near the entrance, where an old jeep was parked. The two buffaloes donated by the police officer—now multiplied into several—lounged about beneath the keekar. An ordinary rural mid-morning, which was soon punctuated by the excited barks of Jimmy the dog as farm labourers from other villages dropped in carrying Party flags. Bant was bathed and dressed in a fresh white kurta-pyjama. The jeep which the Party had made available to Bant had been given a wash by his third son Jagjiwan, who also functioned as its unpaid driver.

Harbans, dressed in a printed pink suit, dragged her leg as she went to the room where two beds were placed. Her bad leg, the result of paralytic damage, was aching but that did not dampen her enthusiasm. She pulled out a crisply starched deep red muslin turban from

The Ballad of Bant Singh

underneath the thick cotton mattress where it had been kept to be pressed flat. She and Jagjiwan tied it round Bant's head and he was all dressed and ready to go. Bant's golden brown skin was set off by the red colour of his turban and he was looking his best. Deep black eyes, the kind that look naturally kohl-lined, an aquiline nose, and a firm chin marked his well-shaped face. The sleeves of his kurta hung loose from his amputated arms. He sat with his one weak leg crossed over his other thigh with grace and he bore himself with pride.

Bant was to leave for Mansa and get there by 11 a.m. because a big rally and procession to mark the 103rd birth anniversary of patriot Bhagat Singh was being organized there.

The revolutionary Bhagat Singh is a national icon and, for Punjabis, he is the last of the heroes who evoke unparalleled veneration. His is the kind of fan following enjoyed by saints like Kabir and Nanak and he is owned across religions, sects, classes and ideologies. This is because the sacrifice of one so young, intelligent and handsome, who had everything going for him is not easy to forget. His charisma as well his writing is still a source of inspiration. The gods may or may not love those who die young, but human beings certainly do. When he was hanged in the Lahore Central Jail, along with his comrades Rajguru and Sukhdev, people poured onto the streets spontaneously and women joined the

Song Sung Red

protest singing his wedding songs, as the metaphorical interpretation of his sacrifice was that he had chosen to wed death so that his country could gain freedom. The Hindus love him and so do the Sikhs. The Right claims him and so does the Left. Perhaps the latter claim carries more weight because Bhagat Singh proclaimed himself an atheist and subscribed first to Anarchist and later to Marxist communist ideology.

In the seventies, after the Naxalite uprising had been crushed in Punjab, there was an attempt to give his image a turban to replace the more popular one in which he wears a hat. The Left resisted the attempt to turn Bhagat Singh, a secular hero, into a Sikh hero with support from Singh's nephew Jagmohan. According to Jagmohan, 'Bhagat Singh was a secular man and we did not want him to be limited to just one faith.'

However, what is more pertinent to our story is what Bhagat Singh said on the caste system and untouchability. Writing in *Kirti* in 1929, Bhagat Singh recounted in an essay on untouchability how the efforts of the Naujawan Bharat Sabha to raise awareness among the low castes were countered by government agents who started inciting the Jat community saying that these 'menials' would become so emboldened, they would refuse to serve them. This threat was sufficient to provoke the Jats to oppose any such awareness-raising campaigns. Rubbishing the policy of gradual reform

The Ballad of Bant Singh

Bhagat Singh called out to the oppressed castes to raise the banner of revolt. He wrote:

> Our country is unique where six crore citizens are called untouchables and their mere touch defiles the upper castes. Gods get enraged if they enter the temples. It is shameful that such things are being practiced in the twentieth century. We claim to be a spiritual country but hesitate to accept equality of all human beings while materialist Europe is talking of revolution since centuries. They had proclaimed equality during the American and French revolutions. However, we are still debating whether the untouchable is entitled for the sacred thread or can he read the Vedas or not. We are chagrined about discrimination against Indians in foreign lands, and whine that the English do not give us equal rights in India. Given our conduct, do we really have any right to complain about such matters?
>
> However, ultimately the problem cannot be satisfactorily solved unless and until untouchable communities themselves unite and organise. We regard their recent uniting to form their distinct identity, and also demanding representation equal to Muslims in legislatures, being equal to them in numbers, a move in the right direction. Either reject communal representation altogether, else give these people their due share!

~

Song Sung Red

Bant Singh's sons lifted their father and put him into the jeep. Harbans sat by his side and the youngest son Paroche, who was all of eleven, joined them with a Party flag in hand. The folded wheelchair was placed in the jeep and a few workers squatted in the open space in the rear. The journey to town began with the humming of a revolutionary song mocking the farce of democratic government. It was set to a catchy folk tune:

> Tu nit aakhdi main lokan di, main lokan di
> Tere dekh laye ne thaan thaan kaare
> Assee pahunchna shahidanwali manzil
> Saanu satguru kol jeharhi ni pukare
> Saanu gurhti ditti Baabe Boojhe Sher ne...
>
> You keep saying that you belong to the people
> But your deeds don't support your claims
> We will reach the destination of our martyrs
> The true Guru is calling out to us
> Our guide is Baba Boojha the lion...

The jeep passed by the shabby bazaar area of Mansa and, turning left from the bus stand, stopped outside a building called the Baba Boojha Singh Bhawan. Baba Boojha Singh was a freedom fighter of the Ghadar movement who became one of the leaders of the Naxalite uprising. Naxalite groups claimed that he was the first casualty of the state oppression after he was killed at the age of eighty allegedly in an fake police encounter.

Bant Singh is a popular person among workers; he is

the vice-president of the Mazdoor Mukti Morcha and workers consider him one of them. Sitting in the wheelchair beneath the shady banyan tree in the district courts complex he was surrounded by landless labourers from different villages around Mansa, many of whom he had helped out of bonded labour and other excesses by the Jat landlords. Among those who came up to greet him, waving Party flags, were Seva Singh and Gurjeet Kaur, the Dalit couple of Burj Dhilwan village whom Bant had gone to visit on the ill-fated night of 5 January.

Farm labour in Punjab is part of the unorganized sector and, in the Cotton Belt, there are few alternatives for employment. Scant wages are accompanied by different kinds of exploitation. There have been cases in which Dalit women have had to work as domestic help for as long as twelve to fifteen years without any wages to repay a paltry loan of a thousand or fifteen hundred rupees. Worse still are cases of Dalit men hooked on to opium, a common practice in Punjab in which labourers are given opium and its by-products, like poppy husk, by landlords so that they work continuously for longer hours without feeling fatigue—they are bonded labour working for a daily fix. Such were the lives which Bant and his comrades had been trying to bring some relief to by organizing workers and demanding better wages and living conditions for them. It was little wonder that they became targets for landlords used to having their way for hundreds of years.

Song Sung Red

Workers, young and old, kept pouring into the complex from different villages around Mansa to celebrate Bhagat Singh's birth anniversary. Women and children, too, were part of the gathering. Every worker and every village had a story of struggle to share. They were anxious that minimum wages be implemented at the earliest. One worker, on learning that I was a scribe, wanted to know if I would reach the spot if I were to be informed of some atrocity. I told him that I was no longer a reporter but there were others who could be contacted. Bant explained to him that I would come only if something very big happened. I blushed—it really does take something 'big' for media persons to take notice; media must thrive upon disasters and tragedies.

The volunteers were busy laying out revolutionary posters and books. A microphone was being fixed centre-stage. Tableaux were being prepared for the procession to be taken out through the town and several children and young men were dressed in Bhagat Singh costumes. Inderjeet Singh, a local artist, had designed a new image of Bhagat Singh with a copy of *Das Kapital* in hand as against more recent calendar images showing him with a pistol or a bomb. The image of Bhagat Singh has always symbolized courage, struggle and sacrifice. Christopher Pinney, professor of Anthroplogy and Visual Culture, University College, London, wrote thus: 'Bhagat Singh's popular appeal was (and still is) enormous and this is usually presented as an intriguing anomaly: Jawaharlal Nehru's *Autobiography* is usually cited noting Bhagat's "sudden and amazing popularity".' Bhagat Singh has been the subject of many chromolithographs since 1931 and from 1954 to 2002 as many as seven popular films have been made on his life. There was a particularly eye-catching poster of the martyr at the venue with the catchphrase: 'The sword of revolution is sharpened at the whetstone of thought.'

The artistes among the workers came out to sing spirited songs and Ajmer Aklia set the mood by singing a ghodhi, a marriage song, about Bhagat Singh composed by an anonymous woman which called out to all women to sing the ghodhi of the one who dies a million times fighting for justice. More songs followed and also a satirical street play on politicians and the corruption that comes with power. Bhan Singh of Saharana village staged a magic show, popularized by the rationalists' group of Punjab called Tarksheel Society, in which he performed tricks and then demonstrated how he did them to prove that there was no such thing as magic. Then the name of Bant Singh 'Jhabbar'—it is customary to suffix the village's name to a person's name in Punjab—was called and Paroche pushed his wheelchair up to the mic. Bant's soulful voice resounded through the compound. The song he dedicated to Bhagat Singh is by Sant Ram Udasi: 'Maghda rahin ve sooraja tu kamean de veharhe' (*O Sun, keep shining on the tenements of the workers*).

~

After a long day at Mansa, we returned to Bant's home in the village for tea and pakodas before starting the return journey to Chandigarh but more so to share some time with Bant and listen to his stories. Although politically positioned as a Communist, he loves to recount tales of valour from Sikh history; the rich and robust oral tradition of Punjab is part of his inheritance. The stories that find favour with him are those which concern the downtrodden, the lower castes or those who labour hard for a living. This has been the main thrust of his struggle throughout his life. He tells the story of Guru Nanak's love for carpenter Lalo of Eminabad, a town thirty-five kilometres from Lahore, known as Saidpur in medieval times, with great delight: 'You know the great Guru chose to camp there in the hovel of a poor carpenter called Lalo. He shared the dry roti that Lalo ate. Malik Bhago, the rich, upper-caste town chief wished to invite the Guru to a feast. Bhago arranged a brahm bhoj for a hundred people with every kind of delicacy to be served at the grand occasion.

'But you know what Guru Nanak did? He declined the invitation. This annoyed Bhago and he asked the Guru: "Why do you prefer the sukki roti that Lalo gives you to the fine food that I offer you?" The Guru's reply was simple. He said that Lalo earned the coarse bread through honesty and hard work whereas Bhago's rich savouries were the result of the exploitation of the poor. Guru Nanak held that food earned with hard work was like milk and food made from ill-gotten money like blood.

'The great Guru brought about a change of heart in many rich men. Have you heard the qissa of Seth Dunni Chand? Nanak had earned the status of a saint in his lifetime and wealthy men wanted his blessings and tried to press costly gifts upon him. Dunni Chand was doing the same. The Guru pulled out a needle from his pocket and asked him to return it to him in the next world. At this the Seth laughed and said: "But how will I take this needle to the next world?"

'The Guru then said that this was precisely the point: if a small needle could not make it into the next world, then was there a point in amassing wealth? Wealth was of no use if it could not be shared with the poor. This had such an impact on the Seth that he distributed all his money to the poor.'

These stories from the radical religious past sound ironic in the face of present-day reality. Yet they also illustrate the pride these tales were able to instill in the Mazhabi Sikhs who were considered nothing better than the scum of the earth until kindred souls, trying to establish a just social order, gave them pride of work and a religion that was compassionate. When Bhai Jaita, who is considered the first Dalit poet of Punjabi, was proclaimed a son of the Guru he exclaimed in ecstasy: 'O Jaite, the saviour Guru has saved the ranghretas/ The pure Guru has made us his sons.' Little did Jaita know that it would not be so easy to shake off the shackles of caste.

~

In India, by and large, caste is also class. That is why, even today, the landless upper castes in Punjab have a sense of caste pride, while the Dalit is not allowed pride of any kind.

As Sikh history moved from its theological moorings to monarchy, the radicalism of the Sikh Gurus became diluted and the old order systematically re-established itself.

Gail Omvedt in her remarkable book *Seeking Begampura* traces the persistence of caste among Indians in spite of the efforts of radical saints and great visionaries. Referring to the Bhakti movement in Maharashtra and Punjab, she writes: 'The bhakti movements, which had earlier local and regional roots but a pan-regional scope, ended by feeding into regional-nationalist unities that were embodied by landed elites asserting themselves against the higher imperial power.

The Ballad of Bant Singh

But in doing so they were co-opted, distorted and sanitised. The landed elites benefited from bhakti equality, but denied these benefits to the subaltern toilers. Thus, for example, the Sikh kingdom saw a resurgence of Jat power but Mazhabi Sikhs (converts from untouchables) continued to be viewed as low.'

Paradoxically, the 'Brahmanisation' of the Sikh religion was to happen during the much-extolled reign of Maharaja Ranjit Singh (1780-1839). The Jat Maharaja issued coins in the name of the first and the tenth Sikh Gurus on assuming the title of Maharaja of Punjab. The Persian verse inscription read:

> My largesse, my victories, my unalloyed fame
> I owe to Guru Nanak and Guru Gobind Singh

This was a humble dedication but that was perhaps the beginning of the erosion of the casteless and egalitarian faith so painstakingly founded by the Sikh Gurus. The very title of maharaja that he assumed was contrary to the teachings of the Gurus and had its roots in the ancient Hindu monarchical order. Even his coronation was performed in the Hindu tradition with the family priest, a Brahmin purohit, applying the vermilion raj tilak on his head and proclaiming him emperor. The last journey of the first Sikh emperor saw four of his queens and seven slave girls burn themselves along with his remains in the Hindu practice of Sati, which the third Guru, Amar Das (1552-1574), had prohibited. An early historian, Syed Muhammad Latif, in his *History of the Panjab*, first published in 1899, takes vicarious pleasure in describing the funeral in macabre detail:

> Four of the Maharaja's *Ranis* and seven of his slave girls, of their own free will and accord, prepared to burn themselves along with the body of their lord and husband, animated with the hope given them by their religion, of entering paradise along with their earthly master...
>
> ...The four *ranis* with death-despising intrepidity, then ascended the fatal ladder, one by one, according to their rank, and occupied a place at the head of their royal husband, holding the head with their hands. The slave girls with equal courage and contempt for death, then ascended the ladder and placed themselves at the foot of their lord...'

According to an eyewitness account, described in *History of the Panjab*, a thick reed mat, soaked in oil, was placed on them all. Oil, attar and ghee were then poured and Prince Kharak Singh lit the pyre. The corpse of the Maharaja and the eleven satis went up in flames.

Maharaja Ranjit Singh was an astute ruler and, to hold his vast kingdom together, he chose advisors and confidants from among the non-Sikhs, too, and Hindus were in the first file. To put down internal rivalries and conflicts, he chose, for his inner council, individuals whose status had been conferred upon them by him and who would remain loyal at any cost. He also did away with the Sikh polity, the gurumata, in which collective sanction was taken from the Sarbat Khalsa—a large congregation of Sikhs. He relied on a few trusted advisers. The republican practice of Guru Gobind Singh was replaced by a monarchical tradition.

The Sikh Gurus had inducted a large number of the Jats into their fold, farmers who were not part of the classified Hindu caste system. The Jats became a powerful force in Punjab, and with the rise of one of them to the position of emperor, they constituted a major part of the nobility and were the greatest beneficiaries of jagirs or land grants. The Jat supremacy in Punjab was further strengthened by the British rulers after their annexation of Punjab in 1849.

The lower castes were bogged down in menial work and untouchability was practised in the Sikh kingdom. This was the period when care of the gurudwaras passed on to Khatri mahants. The Mazhabi Sikhs were referred to as the Chautha Paurha (the fourth step)—they were not allowed beyond the fourth step of the stairs leading up to Harmandir Sahib in Amritsar. Within a century of the death of the tenth Guru, all the abhorred Hindu rites and rituals were back in practice and the faith was gradually moving towards the Sanatan Sikhism of the nineteenth and early-twentieth centuries.

Song Sung Red

There is a heart-wrenching eyewitness account of the fate of a Mazhabi Sikh who dared go beyond the fourth step to mix with other Sikhs and partake of the langar in the *Bansavalinama Dasan Patshaheean Ka*, an eighteenth-century genealogical account of the ten Sikh Gurus, penned by Bhai Kesar Singh Chibber. Chibber was a Brahmin poet-historian who embraced Sikhism and wrote copious praise of the Sikh Gurus and the new faith. This incident illustrates the position of the Dalits within just ten years of the passing away of Guru Gobind Singh.

In the account, an influential religious person, Kahan Singh Trehan, spots a Mazhabi Sikh mixing with other Sikhs and eating with them. The Dalit's hair is shaved off, then he is paraded through town on donkey-back and then hanged.

Referring to this graphic account, Harish Puri, political analyst and scholar of Dalit studies, comments:

> It is commonly believed that a kind of Brahmanisation of Sikh religion started with Maharaja Ranjit Singh, as if between 1699 and 1799, the community had been so transformed as to be free of caste differences. That kind of radical transformation of social mind does not happen merely on the teachings and dictates of a Guru or a great Saint. It is a process that works through persistent practice of a discipline and internal contestation and resistance over a long period. The

main character in the story is Kahan Singh Trehan, a descendent of Guru Angad Dev and a contemporary of Guru Gobind Singh and one very close to Banda Bahadur. And you come to know about the ruling world view of the ruling religious persons and how a low caste Sikh was dealt with for daring to enter there.

Rajkumar Hans writes in his paper, 'Dalits and the Emancipatory Sikh Religion':

> The Ranghretas/Mazhabis had offered numerically critical support in Guru Gobind Singh's battles. So much so that by the mid-eighteenth century when, amidst sustained persecutions by the Mughals, the Sikhs organised themselves into five dals (warrior bands) one of these was Mazhbi/Ranghreta dal under the command of Bir Singh Ranghreta who had a 1300-horsemen force. Throughout the eighteenth century the Dalit military force played a very important role in consolidating the Sikh power. Most of Akali Nihangs were constituted by Dalit manpower and they had assumed deadening military power.

However Bir Singh, according to a historical account by Naranjan Arifi, came to a sad end. Charat Singh, the grandfather of Ranjit Singh, is said to have invited him to Amritsar. When he was taken to Darbar Sahib, he was asked to disarm himself and his soldiers asked to pay obeisance; they were then treacherously killed. After that, Mazhabis remained only in subordinate positions in different misals.

~

After the stories of the Gurus, Bant returned to the sacrifice of Bhagat Singh. He said, 'Our tragedy is that there are no Bhagat Singhs among us. Young, handsome, wealthy and educated, he laid down his life for the nation. He fought British imperialism at the cost of his own life. The leaders today are black imperialists. Nothing good will come from these kale Angrez.'

The Inheritance of Caste

When penury does not chase us
When we get to know well-being
Then it will be a happy Diwali!

—Udasi

IN 2011, THE festival of Diwali was more than a month away but Bant Singh's sons had already started finding ways of earning money so that they could celebrate it well. The second son, Jagjiwan, who drove the jeep given by the Party to Bant, was doing night shifts at a nearby rice-mill for which he received two hundred rupees as daily wages. The eldest, Nirbhay, worked as a labourer in a factory in Bathinda and came home just once a week. The third son, Manjit, who did well academically and was a fitness freak, had planted marigolds in pots made out of plastic waste. The youngest, Paroche, the darling of the family, was most excited. During the school holidays he had picked cotton in the fields of a friendly landlord and returned home before sunset with seventy-five rupees for fireworks. His elder sister Hardeep teased him, 'Well, Paroche, you are a rich fellow today!'

'I was a little girl when he was born,' said Hardeep to me, 'I looked at him and said, here, Paroche has arrived. Since then this has been his nickname.'

'Before becoming followers of Sikhism, we were from the lineage of Balmiki, just as chamars are from the

The Ballad of Bant Singh

lineage of Ravi Das,' Bant told me, tracing his lineage in the context of the festival of Diwali.

Rishi Valmiki—or Balmiki as the name is pronounced by Punjabis—who is described by sociologist Mark Juergensmeyer as the 'Saint of the Sweepers', was from a low-caste background. He attained emancipation by raising his spiritual powers and gaining mastery over the Sanskrit language. A contemporary of Rama, he is considered the author of the original epic of Ramayana, which is also known as the *Balmiki Ramayana*. It was in his hermitage that Sita sought refuge and gave birth to Lav and Kush.

The Balmikis are a prominent Dalit community in Punjab, and were an offshoot of the Adi Dharam movement of the early twentieth century, which was an effort to give the lowest castes a sense of identity. The Balmikis believe both in the Adi Granth of the Sikhs and in the Ramayana. They celebrate both Sikh and Hindu festivals.

Religious traditions in Punjab have always been the meeting place of many cultures and have never been rigid. Hindus and Sikhs throng to the mazaars of Sufi saints and members of these two communities far outnumber Muslim devotees at Hyder Shah's dargah in Malerkotla in Punjab. Everyone visits mazaars, samadhis or deras.

A good instance of fluidity in religious approach in

The Inheritance of Caste

Punjab—on both sides of the border—can be seen in the buses which ply there. Each vehicle is decorated with many icons. Of course, the images of the first and the tenth Sikh Gurus will be present, along with one picture of Bhagat Singh and, in all probability, a picture of the Sufi poet Sheikh Baba Farid. Alongside will be a picture of the living guru of one of the deras as well as one of the incarnations of Durga. An excellent illustration of playing safe the Punjabi way.

Akram Varriach, a Lahore-based painter-poet, further illustrated the tolerant ways of the Punjabis during a conversation with me. Varraich specializes in painting and photographing derelict temples and gurudwaras in an attempt to preserve what he can of a lost composite culture. While photographing a small picturesque temple in Baddo di Gosain village on the banks of the Chenab River from afar, he said that he and his friends were tempted to light a lamp there one day. 'We went there one day to do so and to our surprise we found a lamp already lit. Since there were no Hindus in the vicinity, some Muslim must have done it,' recounted Varraich. 'Our curiosity took us there several times and each time we found a lit lamp.'

In the legend of Heer-Ranjha, Ranjha, a Muslim, becomes a yogi pining for his beloved. Also well known is the love Sufi poet Shah Husain had for his Hindu friend Madho Lal. His love was so great that Husain even started calling himself Madho Lal.

The Ballad of Bant Singh

However, despite a degree of religious fluidity, caste prejudice continues—even in the Muslim-majority Punjab province of Pakistan. This is reflected in the literature from the region. Major Ishaq Mohammad, founding president of the Mazdoor Kissan Party (MKP) and a revolutionary thinker, poet and playwright, wrote the renowned play *Musalli* when in jail—he had been imprisoned for his involvement in the Rawalpindi Conspiracy Case—which chronicled the deeply rooted apartheid in Pakistani Punjabi society, a fact that many Pakistanis are loath to admit because they believe that Muslims cannot possibly practise discrimination along caste lines.

Raza Rumi, a popular online columnist, writes:

> Who said casteism was extinct in Pakistan? My friends have not been allowed to marry outside their caste or sect, Christian servants in Pakistani households are not permitted to touch kitchen utensils, and the word 'Choorha' is the ultimate insult after the ritualistic out-of wedlock sex and incestuous abuses involving mothers and sisters or their unmentionable anatomical parts. The untouchables of the cities and the villages are called something else but they remain the underbelly of our existence. Admittedly these incidences are on a lesser scale than in India. That simply is a function of demographics. Even Mohammad Iqbal, the great reformist poet, lamented in one of his couplets: *Yun tau Syed bhi ho, Mirza bhi*

ho, Afghan bhi ho/Tum sabhi kuch ho, batao tau Mussalman bhi ho (You are Syeds, Mirzas and Afghans/You are everything but Muslims).

Mohammed Hanif, a major writer from Pakistan, in his second novel, *Our Lady of Alice Bhatti*, takes his protagonists from the lowest of the castes who have converted to Christianity but attempt to hide it because that will lay bare their identity.

The word commonly used for the women members of the scavenger community is mehtarani. Delhi-based painter Gogi Saroj Pal recounted visiting Lahore in the eighties where she was put up as a guest in a household in the inner city. After cleaning the bathroom and washing the clothes, the mehtarani came to Gogi and asked her if she had come from India. Gogi replied in the affirmative but wanted to know how the woman had guessed it.

'I saw the label on your kurta and the Hindi written on it.'

'You know Hindi?'

'Yes, before the Partition of the country we were a part of the Hindu religion.'

'Why did you not migrate at the time of the Partition?'

The mehtarani laughed and replied, 'What difference would it have made to us? We clean shit here and we would have cleaned shit there.'

~

The Ballad of Bant Singh

The Hindu caste system originated with lawgiver Manu, from rules clearly laid out in his book, *Manusmriti*, estimated to have been written some two hundred years before Christ. Manu divided society into four varnas or social classes. At the top were the Brahmins who were the scholars and the clergy. Next came the Kshatriyas, who were the kings, warriors and administrators. On the third rung were the Vaishyas, who were agriculturalists, artisans and merchants. The fourth and the most discriminated-against class was that of Shudras or labourers.

According to the *Manusmriti*, the Shudra was deemed impure and therefore no sacred act should be performed within his sight and within his hearing. He was not to be given the respect and regard that was the privilege of the other classes. The life of a member of this class was worth little, so anyone from the upper caste could kill him and the compensation the killer would have to pay was just a fraction of what he would have to pay had he killed a member of one of the other castes. A member of the fourth caste was forbidden to acquire knowledge and it was considered a criminal offence if anyone dared to impart education to him. The Shudra could not own any property or hold any office in the state. The duty of the Shudra as well as his salvation lay in serving the upper castes. The members of the upper caste could not marry a Shudra but they could keep a Shudra woman as a mistress. However, if a Shudra man touched a woman of an upper caste he would have to pay for it with his life. The higher castes were to give their leftover food, castaway clothes, the remnants of their grain and broken utensils, as well as other household goods, to Shudras. The Shudras were forced to live outside the village, near burial grounds or certain identified trees. Thousands of years after the *Manusmriti* was written and adopted, and when the world has progressed so much and India is counted as a country of the future, nothing much seems to have changed for the downtrodden.

Gurdas Singh Gharu, the elder brother of the poet Udasi says about the Dalits of Punjab:

> We could not touch the utensils of the Jats because these would thus get polluted. We could not drink water from the village well. We could only drink from a flowing stream. The Dalit women would sweep, clean and make dung fuel for the Jat households. The Dalits were so afraid that they would not take water from cans kept by the wells in the summers. We would work in the sun and wait for some member of the upper caste to pass by and pour out the water for us otherwise we would remain thirsty. The Dalits had to do share cropping with the Jats and get one-fifth of the share but debts taken at the time of weddings could not be paid off and generations were caught in bonded labour.

Independence too did not change much in practice for a majority of Dalits.

While the caste system was created by Brahmins, in Punjab it has always been reinforced by the Jats, the dominant land-owning class. According to the British archaeologist Alexander Cunningham as well as James Tod, an officer of the East India Company and scholar, Jats were nomadic tribes of Indo-Scythian origin who later became a caste. The American scholar Mark Juergensmeyer says: 'The presence of Jats modified the traditional caste structure by introducing another in which a large cluster of Jat sub-castes were surrounded by a variety of servant and merchant castes.'

Sandhu—Punjabi short-fiction writer Gulzar Sandhu, who is a Jat by caste—and his doctor wife Surjit explained to me how Jats would establish a Punjabi village. 'The Jats would demarcate an area to start farming and then they would bring members of other castes to do related work: a carpenter, a teli or oil extractor, a water carrier, scavengers and a priest,' said Sandhu. 'It was only when I went to the South did I realize that a Bahman (Brahmin) was such an important caste because in the Punjab villages he was a menial like others. He was required for the rituals of birth and death but was addressed with contempt as the Bahman kutta (dog).'

Thus the study of caste becomes curious in Punjab,

with the Brahmins enjoying little or no power and with the very foundation of Sikhism negating caste. It becomes curiouser when one considers that it is the Jats who are the most aggressive upholders of Sikhism.

Prakash Tandon in his book *Punjabi Century*, tracing the history of his family from 1857—the year of the First War of Independence from British colonial rule—to the Partition in 1947, paints a pathetic picture of Brahmins in villages in Punjab:

> With us brahmins were an underprivileged class and exercised little or no influence on the community. Perhaps Muslims had so discouraged temples and external worship that the Brahmins had no place left from where to exercise their authority.
>
> Our brahmins did not as a rule even have the role of teachers, because until the British opened regular schools teaching was done by Muslim mullahs in the mosques or by Sikh granthis…in the gurudwaras. Our Brahmins were rarely erudite; in fact many of them were barely literate, possessing only a perfunctory knowledge of rituals and knowing just the necessary mantras by heart.

According to the scholar Harish K. Puri:

> Brahmins are at the top in Hindu Caste hierarchy. Among the Sikhs, on the other hand, Jats who had graduated to the position of a ruling class under Maharaja Ranjit Singh, came on the top of the

hierarchy. Generally speaking, Khatris, Aroras and Labanas came after them, followed by the artisan castes among whom Ramgarhias (Sikh Carpenter caste) enjoy higher status than Ahluwalias (*kalals*). The menial or untouchable castes are at the bottom, just as among the Hindus.

~

While 'untouchability' was never as visible in Punjab as it was in other states of India, the 'hidden apartheid' has had a long innings in the state. The two castes that were always considered 'untouchable' were the Chamar (tanners) and the Choohra (scavengers). The legend about the former is that Chanu and Banu were two merchant brothers from the Bania caste. Chanu skinned a dead animal and sold it. He was thus rendered an outcaste. The fifteenth-century saint, Guru Ravidas, believed to be a descendant of Chanu, was a mystic saint of the Bhakti movement. His verses and hymns had a great impact on people and forty of them are included in the *Adi Granth* of the Sikhs. In the late nineteenth and early twentieth centuries there emerged a strong Ravidasia movement by the Punjab Chamars who regard him as their Guru, much to the annoyance of the Sikh mainstream. However, this caste, especially in the Doaba region, has improved its economic status over time. Many members own industrial units in and around

The Inheritance of Caste

Jalandhar and also have a strong presence among the Punjabi diaspora.

But this ray of hope is yet to come to the Choorha community. According to Rahi, 'My community can well be called the Dalits of the Dalits, for they face oppression even from the oppressed. Not only do the upper castes discriminate against them, but even some of the lower castes do the same. The affluence that has come to a section of the Ravidasias eludes them because they form a part of the unskilled labour who are sweepers in the towns and agrarian labourers in the villages.' There has been no economic uplift for the majority. It is this caste that also constitutes the Mazhabi Sikhs.

Historically, it was the British annexation of Punjab in 1849 which led to major changes in caste hierarchies. The new masters wanted new loyalties. Sikh soldiers were dispersed and the large landholdings of many prominent chiefs were taken over. For instance Jawahar Singh, son of Hari Singh Nalwa, the commander-in-chief of the Sikh empire, known for his great conquests, had to forego his jagir and was not even given a pension. The recruitment of the Sikhs, considered excellent warriors by the British, increased. The First War of Independence in 1857—called the Sepoy Mutiny by the British—found Sikh soldiers on the side of the British. A year later, the Sikhs, primarily Jats, constituted twenty-eight per cent of the army in Punjab. This was seen by many historians as a reward for their steadfast loyalty. It is significant to note that the British directive for the recruitment to the army was: 'No Sikh is to be required either to cut either his hair or his beard, and all who enter the service with kes are to be required to continue to wear the hair after that fashion.' The order by the commander-in-chief was that every effort should be made to preserve the distinct character of this community, as it was relatively free from caste prejudices. This was a time when more Dalits stepped into the Mazhabi Sikh fold because it meant enlistment in the army and a livelihood; it was essential to write the name of one's religion to enlist and Mazhabi Sikhs were freely enlisted in the army.

The British became acquainted with the fighting ability of the Mazhabi soldiers during the Anglo-Sikh wars. They were impressed by their capacity to sustain themselves on very little—the result of having survived thousands of years of want and oppression! The Corps of Mazhabi Sikh Pioneers, forerunners of the Sikh Light Infantry, was raised in 1850. Initially their services were used for road construction but, in 1857, twelve thousand Mazhabis were recruited for the 23rd, 32nd and 34th Pioneer Regiments. They were deployed against the 'rebels' during the Siege of Delhi, the Siege of Lucknow and the Capture of Lucknow.

However, the status of the Mazhabis, which the

recognition given them by the British had raised, received a setback when the British began developing the nine Canal Colonies between 1885 and 1940. As part of the development, forty lakh acres of virgin land was allocated among dominant castes, mainly the Jats. As always, lower castes such as the Mazhabis, Balmikis and Ravidasias were debarred from owning land. Even village commons could be shared only by traditionally landowning communities. The British stuck to the status quo so as to not upset the social and economic order.

Mazhabi Sikhs lived in a cluster of mud huts on a patch of land called, derogatively, thathi or chamrali. An official document dated 1914-15, while listing the abominably low customary compensation for the backward castes, states that the Choorhas and Chamars worked for free and were only given dead animals in return. These were agrarian labourers doing the hardest work as compared to carpenters, potters, ironsmiths, washermen or barbers, who did receive a marginal share of grain.

The scarcity of space for the fourth caste was appalling, especially when one considers the sprawling acres of cultivated and uncultivated land that were available. Punjabi poet Balbir Madhopuri, in his autobiography, *Chhangya Rukh* (The Shorn Tree) expresses thus the experience of landlessness: 'The "Untouchables" lived on the mercy of the jagirdars and landlords and fear was their constant companion. This was also the reason for their exploitation which included forced free labour. Any refusal would lead to their physical abuse.' Madhopuri also recalls a poignant incident from his childhood. One day he found a young mango sapling by a pond. He carefully dug it out and when he was about to plant it in the vehra his father snatched it from him. Cursing his son, he said: 'So you are trying to copy the Jats? They have havelis spread over six canals. We have only this little space for ourselves. There is no room here for a tree.'

Anguished, the poet says, 'My heart too started withering like the mango sapling. A storm seemed to have shaken off the blossoms of my desires all too soon. I just wanted that our vehra should also have a tree that would attract sparrows, doves and parrots to its branches.'

There is very little space even now. Especially in the Cotton Belt where the landholdings are large, Dalits have little by way of urban opportunities and are compelled to work as agrarian labourers. Their condition depends on the geography and economy of the area where they live, as well as what percentage they form of the total population and what their distribution is. The Doaba region of Punjab—which falls between the Sutlej and Beas rivers—has seen urbanization, has industry and a higher percentage of Dalits, and their conditions have changed for the better. However, a classic example of the yawning gap between the haves and the have-nots is to be seen in the much-touted model village of Badal, in Muktsar district. Badal is also the native village of the Badals, the politically prominent Jat family.

I first visited Badal nearly a decade and a half ago. The vehra in the village presented an awful sight. Debris was piled near overcrowded tenements and all the sewage was collected in an open pond. There was no effort to spruce up the environs, even at election time. In a more recent visit to the village, I found that there has been much development since the time I first went to Badal. There was a B.Ed college, a fancy day school, an upcoming international school, an old-age home and a plush guest house that rarely has any guests. The political heir to the ruling Badal family, Sukhbir Badal, had also built himself a huge, grotesque fortress. The vehra in Badal remained as it always was.

~

Since the nineteenth century, many reforms swept India and the Sikh community in Punjab was no exception. In 1873, the Sri Guru Singh Sabha was set up in Amritsar to encourage the study of the Gurmukhi language and the Sikh scriptures. In 1879 a Singh Sabha was established in Lahore and it had similar objectives. The two sabhas were then merged under the Chief Khalsa

The Ballad of Bant Singh

Diwan in 1903, which paved the way for the setting up of the Shiromani Gurudwara Parbandhak Committee (SGPC) in the 1920s. In the SGPC, reservations were made for the Dalits. The SGPC was itself set up after the Akali movement—also known as the Gurudwara Reform Movement—succeeded in ousting the mahants who had until then controlled the gurudwaras. Harish K. Puri writes in his paper 'The Scheduled Castes in the Sikh Community—A Historical Perspective': 'Priests, ragis and sewadars (as employees) now largely come from the lower castes, including a noticeable number from the Scheduled Castes; and, it may be surprising, fewer from the Jat caste. Jat Sikhs would rather control the Shiromani Gurudwara Parbandhak Committee.'

However, an unfortunate fallout of the reform movement was that another set of Dalits, the Muslim mirasis, who traced their lineage to Mardana, the rabab player and constant companion to Nanak, were ousted from the gurudwaras. With them went the rabab and a very soulful tradition of music. Descendants of these rababis, who once sang the gurbani, today live in poverty in Pakistan where they are doubly out of favour; first, for being musicians, which is considered by some to be un-Islamic and, secondly, for singing hymns written by kafirs. Of course, they are low-caste too.

As the twentieth century progressed, the reform movements gathered pace, but the situation vis-à-vis caste remained vitiated. During the elections of the SGPC, which was also a political body, candidates freely sought votes on the basis of caste. Rajkumar Hans quotes an article from a 1936 issue of the newsletter *Khalsa Sewak* which thus describes the election scenario: 'There was vanity, jealousy and ego clashes all around. Vote-seeking agents did not have anything to sell except caste. Caste names like Saini, Jutt, Rore, Tarkhan, Chamar, etc were being used quite derogatively.' Votes and caste have a history of going hand-in-hand.

Even as all this was going on, the conversions of Dalits had begun much earlier. A Dalit named Ditt was baptised in Sialkot in 1873 and even Christian missionaries were taken by surprise when thousands from the lower castes followed. This led to panic among the Hindus and the Sikhs. Soon after the conversion, the Hindu Arya Samaj stepped up its ritual of shuddhi—purification—while the Singh Sabha began turning its attention to the lower castes.

This period also saw the growing popularity of the Adi Dharam movement across India. In Punjab, the movement was given impetus by a group of educated and reasonably well-off men of the Chamar caste from the Doaba region: Vasant Rai, Thakar Chand and Swami Shudranand. The Doaba region has always had the largest concentration of Dalits. This region is characterized by small landholdings and a higher rate of education and immigration than the rest of Punjab. The freedom fighters—the Ghadari Babas—of the Ghadar Party, founded in Canada and the US in 1913 to liberate India from colonial rule, were from this region. One of the Ghadari Babas was a Dalit man called Babu Mangu Ram Mugowalia.

Mangu Ram was from Mugowal village near Mahilpur in the district of Hoshiarpur. A bright boy whose father had established a successful leather business, he nevertheless had to sit in the doorway of his class in the village school. Yet he passed out from school with distinction. When Mangu Ram was in his early twenties he moved to California in 1909 and worked in the orchard of a Jat Sikh farmer. There he came in contact with the Ghadar activists and became a part of the movement, travelling far and wide. After many adventures and misadventures he finally returned to India in 1925. He set up a school in his village with the help of the Arya Samaj, a school where Dalit children would not have to sit in doorways. When the founder trio of the Adi Dharam approached him, he joined them after some initial hesitation. Mark Juergensmeyer describes him as a twentieth-century hero for Punjabi Dalits:

> Mangoo Ram's Ghadar adventures make an exciting story, but one hesitates to leap to any conclusions about their significance for the Adi Dharam

movement. After all, Mangoo was the only one among his peers who had experienced these things, and the strength of his leadership depended on their fascination than on his ability to speak to the condition of his fellow Punjabis. Still, the American hegira made Mangoo Ram special: the lower castes of Punjab could boast about very few heroes of national—let alone international proportions... For sixteen years abroad he had enjoyed a life in which he was treated as an individual rather than as a Chamar.

The Adi Dharamis rejected all upper-caste saints and texts, and declared that all their saints were Dalit. Besides Guru Ravidas, they claimed the gurus Namdev, Kabir, Valmiki and all other Dalit saints for themselves and, for the first time, established a separate Dalit religious identity. They also approached Sant Sarwan Dass of the Dera Sachkhand, founded by followers of Ravidas in Ballan near Jalandhar to put together the hymns of Guru Ravidas. The *Ad Prakash* was the result, a compendium of the hymns of Ravidas as well as other gurus. The Dera has to its credit the building of the 'Shri Guru Ravidass Janam Asthan Mandir' at Guru Ravidas's birthplace in Seer Goverdhanpur in Varanasi. Built with the help of Dalits from India and abroad, it has millions of devotees from all over the country visiting it. Today it can well be called the Mecca of the Ravidasias.

In 2009 this Dera made international news when

armed assailants killed a Dera preacher, Sant Ramanand, and injured the present Dera head, Sant Niranjan Das, in a Ravidasi Gurudwara at Vienna in Austria. The Sikhs had been protesting Ravidas being called a 'Guru' while the Sikh religion refers to him as 'bhakta'. The violence in Vienna resulted in passionate protests by the Ravidasias in Punjab. Yet another consequence was the decision of Dera Sach Khand Ballan and some others to break away from Sikhism and establish a new faith based entirely on the hymns of Ravidas which have been collected in the *Amrit Bani Granth*. The dominant Sikh clergy as well as fundamentalist groups have been vehemently opposing this, but Dalit scholars point out that the dera is not a Sikh institution and the Sikh code cannot be applied to them. They follow only Ravidas.

It was in 2003 that Des Raj Kali, a Dalit writer-journalist and friend, had taken me to the Dera in Ballan for the first time. At that time he was assisting Harish K. Puri in researching the effect of these Deras on the Dalit psyche. It was an impressive building and the preacher gave us literature on Ravidas. While we were there, some Dalit youths arrived to collect stickers for their motorcycles from the Dera. The slogan on the sticker was 'Saau putt Chamaran de' (Gentle are the sons of Chamars) as opposed to the popular song celebrating the superiority and aggression of the Jat youths, 'Putt jattan de bulavan bakre' (The sons of Jats roar with abandon). I have one lasting image of that visit: a bicycle in the huge covered two-wheeler parking lot. A shoeshine box as well as other items of the man's trade were tied to the bicycle. In which other religious institution could could he so confidently and openly declare his 'untouchable' caste?

~

However, Dalit assertion and resistance have also led to an increase in atrocities on them. This is best illustrated by the conflict over the Talhan shrine between the Jats and the Dalits. Talhan, a village near Jalandhar, made news in 2003 when the Dalit community of Chamars sought a share in the management of the tomb of Shaheed Baba Nihal Singh. Interestingly, this Baba was not a religious preacher like many in Punjab, but a skilled artisan of the Ramgarhia caste from the neighbouring village of Dakoah, who had died while fixing a wheel in a newly dug well near Talhan some years after Independence. In appreciation of his skills, his goodness, and what the villagers counted as the sacrifice of his life while performing a task for the village, he was given the status of a shaheed or martyr—in Punjab there is a passion for martyrdom of any kind—and a tomb was built in his memory. While the Dalits were the more ardent devotees of this shrine, its management was in the hands of the Jat Sikhs. The

The Ballad of Bant Singh

Talhan Dalits gained affluence over the years through employment and business in the sports goods industry of Jalandhar as well as by migrating abroad. They constituted sixty per cent of the five-thousand-strong population of Talhan and contributed a major share of cash offerings, which amounted to between three to seven crore rupees anually. In 2003 the Dalits obtained a court order that they be given representation in the governing committee. The Jat landlords, in collusion with the SGPC, a few radical Sikh organizations, as well as the police and local administration, decided to deny the Dalits any share in the control of the shrine. Overnight, the samadhi was razed to the ground, the picture of Guru Ravidas removed, and a gurudwara was built on the spot, even though the village already had three caste-based gurudwaras.

This led to caste clashes, with the Jalandhar administration playing a biased role in favour of the landlords. But the Dalits of Talhan, many of whom still subscribed to Adi Dharam, were not to be cowed. They fought back with the strength of their numbers and economic self-sufficiency. Adi Dharamis from outside the village, too, participated in the resistance. The Jats declared a boycott of the Dalits but the persistence of the latter in fighting for a rightful share and the media coverage finally led to a compromise. Two Adi Dharamis who wore turbans were to be allowed in the Governing

The Inheritance of Caste

Committee. A public apology was offered by all parties involved in the clashes, the social boycott by the Jats was called off and the photograph of Guru Ravidas was restored.

~

A week or so before Diwali, Gurcharan Singh, Bant's only surviving brother, had an accident and breathed his last.

'Do come for the bhog,' Bant told me, 'you will get to meet my whole clan.'

When I arrived, only Bant and Sukhminder were at home. All others were at the ceremony in the village gurudwara. The bhog was to be followed by a langar so there was no cooking at home. Sukhminder however rustled up some egg bhurji and rotis that Bant and I shared.

Bant wanted to talk. He was bereaved and fond memories stirred within him. How did the accident happen? Gurcharan was walking through the fields, perhaps having had a little too much to drink. He slipped and fell into a deep ditch. The fall disturbed the piles of mud on the brim of the ditch and they fell on top of Gurcharan.

'It took nearly an hour-and-a-half just to pull him out,' said Bant.

As he was telling the story, two elderly women walked

in. One of them covered her face and started wailing and singing an improvised dirge. Bant sat quiet for a while and then consoled the old woman: 'Come Bebe, take a hold of yourself. The one who has gone will not come back.'

He introduced her as Amarjit Kaur, his Bebe, his maternal grandmother. To divert her thoughts he began to talk about his mother. Bebe said, 'She was actually the daughter of my sister-in-law but her parents died when she was very small. We brought her up like our own daughter.'

'Bebe, do I resemble my mother?'

'You are a carbon copy. No other child resembles her as you do. The only difference being that your mother was fair and you are dark. '

'Now don't you go teasing me again, Bebe. I had quite a complex because you called me the dark one in my childhood.'

Bebe, who is light-skinned, laughed. 'Well, a dark one will be called a dark one.'

Slowly, other relatives poured into the house and more charpais were laid out. Baljit and Sukhminder busied themselves making tea. Bant took care to introduce me to Ranjit Kaur, his sister-in-law from Maur Mandi whom he rather fancied as a child. A comely woman in a white suit, she carried herself well and placed her hand on Bant's shoulder by way of sympathy. 'She came as a bride to our home and how all of us adored her,' said Bant.

Bant's sisters were present and, pointing to the older one, a tall graceful woman, he told me: 'This is my eldest siter Bhain Ranjit and it was her bridal dupatta that I had lost when out grazing the goats.'

'Yes, and Bibi had given you a tight slap.'

They were back to their childhood memories, the marbles Bant won from other boys and stored in a glass jar, the game of blind-man's-buff, the box in which Bant had hidden himself after stealing a piece of jaggery from the kitchen. All at once, Roshni, the younger of the two sisters remembered the camel rides.

'Oh! Yes I had forgotten to tell you that my grandfather had a camel on which he would carry fodder and the produce of the Jats to the mandi. The camel had a collar of bells that would jingle. We would love taking rides on it.'

The conversation drifted to Bant's present state and the sisters exclaimed that they had all rushed to the Mansa hospital as soon as they had heard that Bant had been hurt so seriously. 'We are a well-knit family and we always get together in moments of trouble. God has given us trouble aplenty. Wahe Guru baksho (Lord forgive us).' Bhain Ranjit sighed.

Roshni, the more tactless one, added: 'Now look at Bant. What is his life? He is dependent on others for every little need. He is neither dead nor alive. What has he gained by taking on the landlords?'

Bant was silent for a moment and then he said, 'It is only by losing something that we gain something more. I have just lost my limbs. Guru Gobind Singh lost his four sons and Shaheed Bhagat Singh laid down his own life so young...'

All this was lost on the rustic Roshni, who could relate only to the physical distress of her younger brother and not his political struggle for social equality and a life of dignity.

Iconoclast as Icon

Come here, the heir to my songs, lend me a helping hand
I am caught in whirlpools, row my boat to the other end

—Udasi

WHILE EVERY WORKER has inherited Sant Ram Udasi's songs, Bant was to become his real heir. He has not only sung them, but has also translated them into struggle and has imbued them with fresh strength. The working classes, the agrarian labourers, the wretched of the earth are all lovers of the poetic tradition of Udasi, but it is the armless Bant who has braved the whirlpools to take the boat across. Bant cannot read but he knows Udasi's poetry by heart. He is always ready to show off Udasi's book to whoever wants to know about his songs. 'This book has songs on the lives of the poor folk: labourers who till the fields and small farmers who find it difficult to make ends meet. Udasi wrote about their sorrows and struggles but also of their dreams and courage. These are the songs that I sing.'

A comparison between the singer and the writer of the songs is but natural. There are many similarities between Bant and Udasi, and many dissimilarities, too. Both were born into poor Dalit Mazhabi Sikh families, both became activists of the ultra-Left, both had a great voice and a poetic sensibility. Udasi had an education and a calling as a school teacher; Bant never went to school, never learnt to read or write—even though well-meaning Liberation group activists made efforts to make him literate in his long stay at the St. Stephen's Hospital in Delhi. Bant had to take up several callings to fend for himself and his family. Both took recourse to alcohol but, in Udasi's case, it became an addiction. Bant would toil all day and have a couple of drinks before dinner. He still does so and, sharing a drink with me, he says, 'A labourer cannot do without liquor. The fatigue and tensions are such that a few gulps settle him down.' He then laughs. 'It is better than swallowing pesticide as my brother did.' Bant is never without humour, and it is sometimes dark. When some detractors gossiped that Bant had come into money, he laughed and said, 'Well, let them also get their limbs chopped up!'

Udasi was frail in body and suffered from depression in his later years. He was swayed—even though only a little—by the fundamentalist Khalistani movement, and died a sad death while on a train journey. Bant has always remained physically fit and mentally alert, dismisses depression of any kind, and has remained steadfast to his vow of the laal salaam.

However, the one fundamental difference between the two is that Bant has also had to play the role of icon. Journalist Amit Sengupta says, 'In a tangential sense, the ideology of upper-caste domination has been pushed to the wall by Bant Singh's sacrifice and valour. He has

Iconoclast as Icon

become a revolutionary icon, a catalyst for change, a protector of human and fundamental rights, a symbol of defiance against archaic symbols of feudalism and slavery, a physical reality of a dream which is not so impossible.'

Bant plays the part of icon to the hilt, and it is this which keeps him going, no matter what the odds. 'You know, journalists from every country in the world have written my story,' he is fond of claiming. A claim which is not an empty brag because he has indeed been featured—both at home and abroad—in print media as well as in television shows.

In 2011, he was magical on the music stage at the Jaipur Literature Festival, where he performed after the Pakistani pop band Junoon, and sang song after song by Udasi to a young crowd. In the curtain-raiser to the 2011 festival, in a piece titled 'Six of the Best Bets', Nilanjana S. Roy wrote: 'Some day, a folk poet will write the story of Bant Singh into legend. Until then, he'll sing it himself. Singh, a fan of Sant Ram Udasi, is now a fiery protest poet, the resonance and depth in his voice untouched by the violence.' However, there were misgivings before Bant's performance. Some supporters of Bant wondered if he would become a spectacle of sorts: a variety of the 'maimed performing beggar'.

With a little trepidation, I shouted a couple of sentences by way of introduction before Bant came on

The Ballad of Bant Singh

stage—for in the three years of penning his 'ballad' Bant has given me the roles of journalist-on-call, friend and spokesperson—and then disappeared into the crowd in fear of what the response would be like. But the people loved him and gave him due honour and warmth, even when his voice became hoarse. Bant's spirit prevailed, and he was the undisputed star of the evening. In fact Bant was the centre of attraction all day long at Jaipur.

He had travelled from Mansa in a tempo-traveller owned by one of his Party comrades and besides the owner-driver, he travelled with an entourage of six, including his wife, sister, youngest son, his Panchayat-member uncle, another distant relative, and one attendant. The eight of them reached Jaipur in the wee hours but he was at the festival dressed in white and having donned a festive red turban. Many were the questions put to him and he was never at a loss for an answer. When asked to comment on the political system, he said that the lot of the workers could never be bettered unless a Party of the workers, their own Party, came to power. To another query on how he got the courage to fight his oppressors, his reply was: 'I am born to courage for, after all, I am the descendant of Guru Nanak and Guru Gobind Singh.' Bant takes as much pride in being a Communist as he does in being Sikh.

Among those who went to embrace Bant backstage

Iconoclast as Icon

was Mo Dhaliwal, director of the Vancouver International Bhangra Celebration Society, which annually organizes a gala bhangra festival in Canada. Dhaliwal had been long trying to get Bant to the festival. Not an easy task, for Bant did not possess a passport. But when I sent him the invitation verbally, after having received it in writing in an email, his first response was, 'No problems, we will go to Canada too!' But Vancouver is not Jaipur where a tempo-traveller can make it through the night. And, what would Bant's role in a bhangra celebration be? Bhangra, as we see it today, is a merry mix of elements taken from the different folk dances of Punjab and is marked by the macho pride and aggression of the Jat Sikh.

I put my reservations to Dhaliwal and he wrote back:

> The theme of a visit by Bant Singh would be as follows: We are celebrating the work, spirit and perseverance of this revolutionary. Truly, nothing better encapsulates the true Punjabi spirit than 'hass ke qurbani deni (laugh and sacrifice oneself)'... The shock-factor of presenting Bant Singh at these festival events has the potential to send waves through the Indian and the mainstream gora communities in Canada... Such attention puts a lot of focus on human rights and, as you know, when there is a spotlight on [such] matters, change can happen... Bant Singh would inspire and uplift our audiences. True, we are a celebratory event, but celebration doesn't just mean

The Ballad of Bant Singh

singing and dancing. It means having gratitude and appreciating your fellow men.

Dhaliwal's dream has not been realized yet. And, then again, though Dhaliwal does well to talk about Bant being able to inspire and uplift audiences with his indefatigable spirit, it is sad to see a vibrant human being valued for his 'shock-factor'.

~

Bant has a wide and varied range of admirers.

In 2010, three young and hip musicians from Delhi were so inspired by Bant Singh's story that they decided to get to know him and sing with him. Thus began a musical project with Samrat Bhardwaj, Taru Dalmia and Chris Mcguiness. Piling a tempo-traveller with their equipment, they travelled to the 'faraway' village of Jhabbar. Bhardwaj, who performs under the moniker Audio Pervert with the Teddy Boy Kill band, led this odyssey. Dalmia—who goes by the stage name Delhi Sultanate—and DJ McGuiness slept on the rooftop of Bant's house, eating freshly cooked meals and singing along with him, even though they faced a big language gap. Thus were born four bilingual tracks with vocals by Bant Singh and Dalmia and a twelve-minute film called *Word, Sound & Power* which captured the experience of coming together to sing with the revolutionary.

Iconoclast as Icon

Recently, Nicolas Jaoul, a French scholar and a fellow at the Centre National de la Recherche Scientifique (The French National Centre for Scientific Research) who specializes in Dalit studies, was in Jhabbar. What brought him there was a comparative study of two victims of caste violence and the stories of their survival. One was, of course, Bant. The other was Bhaiyalal Bhotmange, a Dalit Buddhist from Kherlanji village in Maharashtra. On 29 September 2006, the same year that Bant was attacked, Bhotmange's family, comprising his wife Surekha, daughter Priyanka, and sons Roshan and Sudhir, were massacred after the women were first gang-raped and grievously tortured by upper-caste men of their village.

Widespread protests by the Dalits followed and eight men were convicted for murder.

Comparing these two cases is not easy, but nevertheless both were clear cases of caste violence. Bhaiyalal lost his entire family and Bant his limbs. While Bant's daughter was raped by two within the walls of a house, Bhaiyalal's wife and daughter were stripped, humiliated and raped by as many as four score men, and all this happened in full view of the villagers, including women. Jaoul says: 'Both these violent acts happened in the same year and what is pertinent to note is that Bant has come out of it stronger than before. Bhaiyalal on the other hand has a government job and is perhaps

The Ballad of Bant Singh

financially better than before but he is a depressed person who has nothing to look forward to in life. The [two cases are] very different and one would like to understand how Bant was able to overcome the atrocities on him and turn into a source of inspiration to others.'

How indeed was Bant able to overcome the brutality? Was it his Leftist political ideology which helped him, or his roots in the militant Sikh tradition? Was it his own unique personality or the campaign led by his Party? (Though there are sections in Punjab which feel that the Party should have taken better care of him as he had been attacked earlier and there was a threat to his life.) And while it was a mix of all of these, it was his own never-say-die spirit which pulled Bant Singh through.

It was Bant's toughness and celebratory spirit which helped him make the personal political. There is a certain grandness in the way in which he lives his life. Nothing exemplified that more than the splendid wedding he arranged for his third daughter, Sukhminder. The Jhabbar village had not seen such an assemblage for a wedding, not even in the homes of the affluent landlords. Over a thousand people came to the feast after the morning wedding in the gurudwara; stalls were set up, offering multi-cuisine delicacies—as happens quite often at urban weddings. And, to top it all, there was an orchestra with dancing girls. This bothered me, for Bant has been vocal at other times in criticizing the orchestras which have Dalit girls dancing in them. When I asked him about it, his reply was: 'Well, everyone wanted an orchestra but I made it clear that the girls would not dance in bikinis but be fully clothed in Punjabi suits.' The wedding was special for Bant. The alliance was to be with a well-off family of Raisar, the village of his beloved poet Udasi. While showing the photographs and videos of this gala event, Bant happily pointed out Sukhminder's marital home. It was as good as a bungalow in the city because Sukhminder's father-in-law was in the construction business. Her husband owned a tractor which he hired out during the farming season. Talking of the wedding, Bant said: 'The boy's side said that they would bring a baarat of three hundred people so I had to call my people, too, and so the gathering numbered a thousand and more.' This is an assertion of Dalit pride even though it runs counter to the Left ideology.

But this is not to say that Bant had taken on the airs of the 'haves'. A year-and-a-half later he arranged the marriage of his eldest son, Nirbhay, with a girl from Raisar, accepting only a rupee from the girl's family as her father was a very poor labourer. It had become important to get Nirbhay married because Sukhminder, who used to perform all the household chores, had left for her in-laws' home.

In fact, very often, a brother and sister are married at the same time so that the household work of the daughter can be taken up by the daughter-in-law. Bant recounted, 'We went to the girl's house and told them about the two things that she would be required to do: hold a tumbler of water to my mouth and feed me.' The girl agreed to both the tasks and then the sweets which the boy's family had brought with them were distributed. Rani, the pretty moon-faced bride, flitted about happily doing her household chores and Bant assured her, 'We are going to get you a bridal lehnga and make a video and take pictures and your wedding will be grand too!'

Bant has a political identity. But he is also a conscientious householder, and the father of eight children, who is called upon all too often to perform a balancing act.

~

Thinking of Bant Singh, Jagseer comes to mind, the Dalit hero who stepped out of Gurdial Singh's first novel *Marhi da Deeva* (translated into English as *The Last Flicker*) in the sixties and walked straight into the hearts of readers, although there was nothing heroic about him. Poverty, an unfulfilled life, unrequited love, addiction to opium and an annoying passivity go into the making of Jagseer. He is an attached Dalit labourer who toils hard like his father for their benevolent landlord Dharam Singh and his son. The betrayal comes when the land given to his father to till—but not transferred to his name courtesy the Land Alienation Act 1900 in which the 'untouchables' were put in the non-agricultural classification and debarred from owning land even though they had long been the tillers of the soil—is snatched away from Jagseer by Dharam Singh's son Bhanta. Jagseer is then thrust into the centre of a changing way of life in which old values are replaced by new greed, and this leads to a slow suicide by the hero who feels insulted and humiliated. His strength lies in bearing all his losses with stoic dignity.

The Dalit hero's story is set in the fifties and the novel first came out in 1964, the post-Nehruvian phase of independent India which had seen many dreams die, including the much-vaunted model of socialism. Jagseer's despondency and death symbolize the mood of the nation then. Hailed as the first Punjabi novel of social realism, and widely translated into Indian and foreign languages, the novel remains till date the most discussed and debated work in Punjabi literature.

From the fictional Jagseer of the fifties of the past century to the real Bant Singh of the first decade of the present century is a long journey, and although the two heroes are diametric opposites in their natures, both their stories underline the crying need for change. The two come from the same Malwa region of Punjab. They belong to the lowest of the low castes, former 'untouchables' who became a part of Sikhism, the religion

The Ballad of Bant Singh

which rejected the practice of the caste system. They also belong to the same class of landless attached labourers who are pitted against 'feudal' lords. Both their stories are entry points to the drama of caste being played out in Punjab where the dominant community of Sikhs, in its philosophy, is supposedly free of the shackles of caste.

In *Marhi da Deeva*, Jagseer is happiest when he is tending to his 'own' fields. The final blow falls upon him when he walks towards 'his own land', to find the tahli tree fallen and chopped up. The whitewashed bricks of his father's tomb, which Jagseer built with his own hands, are scattered and a merchant has arrived to take away the wood. In a sense, *Marhi da Deeva* divines the fate that was to befall Bant Singh some sixty years later. He was beaten to a pulp by the caste descendants of Bhanta and thrown into the fields that once belonged to his grandfather.

However, while the situation vis-a-vis the Dalit and the Jat has not changed much from the time of Jagseer to Bant, the Dalit hero has certainly evolved through awareness and struggle. The fictional protagonist is crushed by the injustice meted out to him, but the real-life hero Bant, a member of a comradeship of labourers organized by the Left, still holds his head high. Jagseer was alone, Bant has his comrades.

Yet I wonder, would there have been a Bant had

Iconoclast as Icon

there been no Jagseer? And while it is true that Jagseer's dreams were crushed, did Gurdial Singh dream that one day a Jagseer would become a Bant? For Bant is the hero today. A hero, I would say, of both the big and the small moments.

~

The last time I met Bant, before wrapping up this book, he was eager that I take a picture of a squirrel with the Party flag. In the long days when Bant sat in the courtyard without meetings, rallies or visitors to keep him occupied, with the members of the family busy with their chores, he only had this squirrel for company. 'I have been watching this squirrel the past few months,' he said, 'and it has been trying to take the Party flag up the tree to build its nest. First I thought I should ask someone to take the flag away from it, but then I decided against it. After all, it is raising our flag high.' I turned to look at the keekar tree to see what Bant was talking about. Indeed, there was a squirrel up in the branches, determined, like King Bruce's spider, to take the flag up to its nest. As I stirred to bring out my camera, it panicked and the flag fell on to a branch below. I let the camera be. And lo, the little squirrel was soon back, tugging at the flag and taking it up to a higher branch. 'Isn't it good to see the flag going up?' Bant said with a smile.

Songs That Bant Sings

Abode of the Labourers

Mother Earth! Many more Moons to your lap
Keep shining, O bright Sun, on the abode of labourers

Where denial is a way of life
Where throats are throttled
Where hair yearns for comb
Noses run, eyes crinkle, teeth grind
Keep shining, O bright Sun, on the abode of labourers

Where the soul is but a ghost
Where life is nothing but regret
Where the lava of pride is dammed
Where the mind is forever abused
Keep shining, O bright Sun, on the abode of labourers

Where the people are truly cut off
Far away from the heart of the Capital
Forever fighting hunger
Where phantoms perform a dance of death
Keep shining, O bright Sun, on the abode of labourers

Where one is born into bonded labour
Where wealth is all-supreme
Where even the unborn are doomed
A son is interest on the father's loan
Keep shining, O bright Sun, on the abode of labourers

They are the ones parched by drought
They are the ones drowned by floods
They are a home for all misery
Where the harvest of labour is gloom
Keep shining, O bright Sun, on the abode of labourers

The Ballad of Bant Singh

Where all roads are shut
Where the dove is beset by crows
Where unwed girls become mothers
Where daughters sigh in grief
Keep shining, O bright Sun, on the abode of labourers

Where the heart is kneaded with flour
Where darkness finds home
Where honour is forever lost
Where vote-seeking leaders make chaos
Keep shining, O bright Sun, on the abode of labourers

You talk always of my and mine
You glorify only yourself
Why do you shy away from workers?
They are condemned to ever remain miserable
Keep shining, O bright Sun, on the abode of labourers

—*Udasi*

Songs That Bant Sings

Diwali

When penury does not chase us
When we get to know well-being
Then it will be a happy Diwali!

When regimes will not dance
   like parasites on green crops
When traitors will not lift
   their heads high
When the festival will not shy
   away from the homes of sages
Then it will be a happy Diwali!

When at the will of a queen
   hundreds of women will not die
When bombs will not be exploded
   to smash the fight for rights
When, buying sweets,
   the purse will not be found empty
Then it will be a happy Diwali!

When brother will not kill brother
   for a throne
When a soldier will not be humiliated
   as a menial in a superior's home

Today it is the festival of tyrants
Tomorrow it will belong to us
Then it will be a happy Diwali!

—*Udasi*

The Ballad of Bant Singh

People's Pledge

Our country is dearer to us than our own life
And the people dearer than the country itself, my friend
We will crush,
We will crush the bloody leech, my friend

When we see lush green fields, we feel pride
We will break your arrogance, O lazy landlord
You will not,
You will not oppress us now, O lazy landlord

When the lions roar, all the cowards will flee
The workers and tillers will not go hungry
Come raise your voice,
Come raise your voice, it is time to be angry

We will bring back the lost spring
People declare, thumping chests, my friend
Who can stop?
Who can stop us now from rising, my friend?

We will be rain for this parched earth
Washing away dust from the storm
We will behead,
We will be behead the century of its gloom

—Udasi

Songs That Bant Sings

Days of Darkness

The goal has not been reached yet, there is a long way to go
Strive still, O tireless traveller, even though the darkness is intense

The image-maker has not printed yet pictures of pain
The blacksmith has not broken yet the shackles of religion
The bowl of love is yet empty, for alms from the beloved
Some Ranjha has come a-begging at humanity's door

Every heart has a grudge, a qualm, every heart is envious
The season is not singing yet, the darkness is intense

The toiling worker goes hungry, the idle get their fill
The mullah, the priest, the granthi, conduct transactions in religion
The human frame is yet in the shadow of feudal lords
The person is yet not in command of destiny

The wretched human form is yet rented out to another
The people have not yet awakened, the darkness is intense

Human dreams and desires are as yet auctioned
For just a paisa or two are faith and scruple still sold

The mountain is as jagged as ever, the axe still blunt
The share-cropper is penniless and the darkness intense
Violence yet roams at will underneath slogans of peace
The world yet goes through hell for the promise of heaven
Dark clouds have not yet made way for a ray of hope
We know mantras yet the poisonous snake roams free

We have yet to tell God that people are stronger than him
The hooter is yet to screech, the darkness is still intense

—Udasi

The Ballad of Bant Singh

A Plea to My Mother

Do not give birth to me in a village where dreams are forever shackled
Where the hot beads of my brother's sweat have no value
Where no tears accompany a couple as they ritually circle to take vows
Where the groom's tinsel-and-flower headgear gives off no sparks
Where dowry follows girls like a deadly infection
A village where, instead of being adorned with gold,
The ears hear only the wails of the wretched, the sick and the hungry

Do not give birth to me in a village where dreams are forever shackled
Where our rights are buried under boulders
Where intellect has long rusted beyond recognition
On the blood-stained wrist, seems to have cracked,
The forlorn glass bangle which met such an end
No one caresses the blossoms on the cotton plants
That seem to be weeping even at full bloom

Do not give birth to me in a village where dreams are forever shackled
In the fat moneylender's ledger, tied with a red ribbon,
The fire of what is rightfully ours lies long imprisoned
Where, kicked by heavy nailed boots in the street,
Our father's turban lies tattered and torn
Our livelihood is cursed says the sigh of a poor woman
Someone else is wrongfully taking our share of the moon
Do not give birth to me in a village where dreams are forever shackled

—Udasi

Songs That Bant Sings

Do Not Weep on My Death

Do not weep on my death, cherish my thoughts
Do not cast the saffron hues of my blood into sand

What was my life, a tall grass in the wilderness
Warm me with your sighs, you need not set me aflame

I do not wish to be imprisoned within four walls
Like my friends, cremate me on the pyre

I do not wish to be reduced to ashes all at once
Whenever the sun sets, burn me bit by bit

Many are the crossroads from life to death
The route that is different, may I be taken that way

—Udasi

Selected Bibliography

Attarjit. *Akk da Dudh* (Poison Milk). Bathinda: Balraj Sahni Prakashan, 2008.

Chibbar, Kesar Singh. *Bansavalinama Dasan Patshaheean Ka*. Edited by Piara Singh Padam. Amritsar: Singh Brothers, 2005.

Dass, Bhagwan. *Main Bhangi Haan*. Translated by Bhagwant Rasulpuri. Nakodar: Bahujan Hit Prakashan, 2006.

Dil, Lal Singh. *Dastaan*. Jalandhar: Lakeer Prakashan, 1998.

Hanif, Mohammed. *Our Lady of Alice Bhatti*. Delhi: Random House, 2011.

Juergensmeyer, Mark. *Religious Rebels in the Punjab: The Ad Dharm Challenge to Caste*. New Delhi: Navayana, 1988.

Latif, Syed Muhammad. *History of the Panjab: From the Remotest History to the Present Time*. Delhi: Kalyani Prakashan, 1994.

Madhopuri, Balbir. *Chhangya Rukh* (The Shorn Tree). Delhi: Navyug, 2003.

Omvedt, Gail. *Seeking Begumpura: The Social Vision of Anticaste Intellectuals*. Delhi: Navayana, 2008.

Puri, Harish K, ed. *Dalits in Regional Context*. Delhi: Rawat Publications, 2004.

Rahi, Rajinder, ed. *Sant Ram Udasi, Sampooran Kavya*. Chandigarh: Lokgeet Parkashan, 2004.

Rasulpuri, Bhagwant. *Main, Shaitan te Indumani*. Jalandhar: Parwaz Parkashan, 1998.

Singh, Gurdial. *Marhi da Deeva*. Delhi: Navyug, 1964.

Singh, Khushwant. *The Sikhs*. Delhi: HarperCollins Publishers, 2006.

Tandon, Prakash. *Punjabi Century: 1857-1947*. California: University of California Press, 1969.

Zaidi, Annie. *Known Turf: Bantering with Bandits and Other True Tales*. Delhi: Tranquebar Press, 2010.

A Word of Thanks

First of all, I heartily thank Bant Singh for opening his home and heart to me. I have also been fortunate enough to have struck up friendships with Harbans, Bant's wife, and their daughters Baljit and Hardeep. Thanks are due to Bant's comrades and mentors Sukhdarshan Natt, Bhagwant Sammaon, Kanwaljit Singh and others for giving me the documents and other inputs which I required. I am grateful to my writer friends Des Raj Kali, Bhagwant Rasoolpuri and Attarjit for their advice, as well as to Megh Raj Mitter and his family for hosting me in Barnala. As also to my young colleagues Vishav Bharti and Neel Kamal for their help. Thanks are due to my brother Vimal for giving the first draft a thorough read and for his valuable suggestions. I am indebted to Professor Harish K. Puri for reading the manuscript, giving it a nod of approval and also for suggesting some new dimensions. Thanks to Professor Raj Kumar Hans for encouraging me in this task. Thanks also to photographer Devinder Singh who drove me to Bant's home to take his pictures. I am grateful to Ravi Singh of Speaking Tiger for keeping faith and publishing *The Ballad of Bant Singh*. And special thanks to Anurag Basnet at Speaking Tiger for his meticulous editing.

www.ingramcontent.com/pod-product-compliance
Lightning Source LLC
Chambersburg PA
CBHW052050220426
43663CB00012B/2510